FINANCIAL LITERACY FOR TEENS AND YOUNG ADULTS 101:

THE ULTIMATE GUIDE TO BUDGET, SAVE AND INVEST MONEY TO BUILD FUTURE WEALTH AND EQUITY AT AN EARLY AGE

EDUARDO HERNANDEZ

CONTENTS

INTRODUCTION

Did you know that over 60% of young adults feel overwhelmed by their financial situation and uncertain about navigating their early financial decisions? This startling fact spotlights the crucial gap our current education system has in preparing you for real-world financial independence.

Let's talk about Alex, a recent college graduate who just received her first paycheck. She's standing in her tiny kitchen, holding the check in one hand and her student loan statement in the other. Should she start chipping away at her debt, or should she put some money into a retirement account, something her friend mentioned but she barely understands? Like many of you, Alex feels thrown into the deep end, expected to make critical financial decisions without a lifeline.

This book is not just a guide, it's your lifeline. It's designed to demystify financial jargon, break down complex concepts, and transform them into practical, easy-to-follow steps specifically for you—the young adults and teens.

Understanding the importance of financial literacy is more than about money; it's about securing your freedom, independence, and long-term peace of mind. This book aims to bridge that gap, providing a clear, engaging pathway through the financial maze of the 21st century.

My journey of overcoming financial illiteracy took work. I stumbled through debts, made uninformed decisions, and learned everything the hard way. These experiences inspired me to ensure that no young adult goes through the same.

Structured to be your go-to guide, this book unfolds in clear, manageable sections. From foundational financial principles and effective money management to the basics of investing and future planning, each part builds on the last. You'll find relatable examples, success stories, and yes, even a few failures to learn from—all complemented by practical tools like worksheets and checklists to bring these lessons to life.

As we move forward, remember this is more than just reading; it's about engaging, questioning, and applying. The principles and advice laid out here are tools at your disposal, but their effectiveness lies in your hands. Embrace this journey with curiosity and dedication, ready to take control of your financial destiny.

Facing financial fears can be daunting, but you're not alone. This book is a conversation, one that I wish I had had years ago. So, let's tackle those fears, step by step, with confidence and a bit of humor, making each financial decision one that leads to greater independence. Ready to start this journey? Let's dive in and make financial literacy your superpower!

CHAPTER 1
UNDERSTANDING YOUR MONEY MINDSET

Ever caught yourself daydreaming about what you'd do if a distant relative left you a staggering inheritance? Maybe you've plotted out your first three purchases or even imagined the type of jet-setting life you'd lead. While this fantasy might seem like a fun escape, it offers a glimpse into your underlying beliefs about money. Yes, how you envision spending an unexpected windfall tells a lot about your financial mindset, which, believe it or not, plays a massive role in your real-life spending, saving, and investing habits.

How we think about money—whether we see it as a tool for freedom, a source of stress, or a pathway to happiness—is often ingrained in us from a young age. These beliefs shape our financial behaviors, sometimes without us realizing it. This chapter will take you on a deep dive into the heart of your financial beliefs, helping you to uncover, understand, and optimize your money mindset for better financial health and independence.

1.1 IDENTIFYING YOUR FINANCIAL BELIEFS AND HOW THEY SHAPE YOUR HABITS

Self-reflection as a Tool

Think back to your earliest memory involving money. Perhaps it was receiving a crisp $10 bill on your birthday or watching your parents argue about a mysterious thing called 'mortgage' or 'bills'. These early experiences start scripting our financial narratives, sketching out what money means to us and how we relate to it.

I encourage you to grab a notebook and jot down these memories and how they made you feel. Did money cause stress or was it a source of joy and possibility? Reflecting on these moments can reveal the foundation of your money habits today. For instance, if you always saw adults stressing over bills, you might have grown up with a scarcity mindset, possibly hoarding every penny or spending money before it seemingly disappears.

Impact of Beliefs on Habits

Your early beliefs about money are like the roots of a tree—they feed and stabilize the growing trunk and branches, representing your financial habits. If you grew up believing that 'money is the root of all evil,' you might subconsciously shy away from opportunities to improve your financial standing, like investing or asking for a raise. On the flip side, seeing money as a tool for achieving dreams and helping others can lead to more positive financial behaviors, like regular saving and ethical investing.

These foundational beliefs impact how you manage your finances, whether you're conscious of it or not. Recognizing the link between your beliefs and habits is the first step to changing your financial narrative.

Changing the Narrative

How do you shift negative money beliefs into positive, empowering ones? Start by challenging these beliefs. Ask yourself, "Is this belief based on truth or my perception?" For example, if you believe you'll never earn enough to save for retirement, challenge this by educating yourself on investment strategies or exploring side hustles that can increase your income.

Replacing old beliefs with fresh, optimistic ones can also reshape your financial habits. Affirm that you can manage your money wisely. Engage with financial education, like this book, and surround yourself with positive influences who encourage perceptive financial decisions. Over time, these new beliefs will form the foundation of healthier financial habits.

The Foundation of Financial Literacy

Understanding and adjusting your money mindset doesn't happen overnight—it's an ongoing process, crucial for achieving financial independence. It's about continually questioning the why behind your financial decisions and aligning your financial practices with your values and goals.

Think of it as setting up a new smartphone. When you first get it, you customize the settings, download your favorite apps, and maybe get a protective case. Similarly, by customizing your financial beliefs to better serve your goals, you supply yourself with a powerful tool—a healthy money mindset—that can protect and prepare you for a prosperous financial future.

In this ever-evolving financial landscape, being aware of and adapting your money mindset is more important than ever. As we move forward, keep this thought in mind: Your financial beliefs don't just influence your current spending, saving, or investing habits—they shape your financial destiny.

1.2 THE PSYCHOLOGY OF SPENDING: WHY WE BUY WHAT WE BUY

Imagine you've had a rough day, and you browse online for items you don't need. It could be a new pair of shoes or the latest technology. Before you know it, you've made a purchase. Sound familiar? This is emotional spending in action—a wallet's worst nightmare. Emotional spending acts as a quick fix to soothe negative feelings. Like eating ice cream straight from the tub when you're feeling down, the relief is temporary and often followed by a dollop of regret. It's driven by various feelings like stress, excitement, or even boredom. Recognizing these emotional triggers is the first step to curb unnecessary spending. Start by asking yourself, "Am I buying this because I need it, or am I trying to fill an emotional void?" Making this distinction can be a game-changer in your spending habits.

Social Media Influence

The influence of our buddies and Instagram feeds, which show the latest dine-outs, exotic vacations, and killer shoes, is strong. It's natural to want to fit in, and this peer pressure can make you spend money to maintain a particular image or lifestyle. It's not just friends; it's the societal expectation set by a culture of consumerism where your worth feels measured by what you own rather than who you are. To combat this, try surrounding yourself with people who share your financial values or those who encourage you to save rather than splurge. Remember, true friends will stick by you whether you sport the latest fashion or rock the classic styles from your existing wardrobe.

Psychological Marketing

Marketing gurus are experts at tapping into our psychological triggers. They use tactics that create a sense of urgency—like limited-time offers or last items in stock—to drive impulsive buying decisions. Ever noticed how sales always seem to end right as you've found out about them? That's no accident. It's a strategy to make you act fast without overthinking whether you need the product. Advertisements also play on your emotions by showing idealized images of happiness, success, and acceptance—all linked to purchasing their products. To shield yourself from these tactics, take a step back and analyze marketing messages. Ask yourself, "Do I want this product because it adds value to my life or because I'm being persuaded to want it?" Being aware of these strategies can help you make more informed, deliberate choices.

So, how do you align your spending with your long-term goals? This is where mindful spending comes into play. Mindful spending isn't about cutting all joys and living like a hermit; it's about ensuring your spending aligns with your true values and long-term objectives. Start by tracking your expenses for a month. You might be surprised to see where your money is going, often on little things that add up. Next, evaluate these expenses against your goals. Does a daily gourmet coffee align with your goal of buying a car or saving for a vacation? If not, what changes can you make to redirect that spending toward your goals? This doesn't mean you can never treat yourself, but rather that when you do, it's done thoughtfully and not out of habit or impulse.

1.3 SETTING FINANCIAL GOALS THAT STICK: DREAMS VS. REALITY

Have you ever set a New Year's resolution to get in shape, read more books, or save money, only to find yourself back to your old habits by February? Setting goals feels like making a pinky promise to yourself that you're half-committed to, but regarding your financial health, setting meaningful and realistic goals isn't just a good idea—it's a necessity. Let's talk about how to set financial goals that inspire you and stick.

What SMART Is

SMART is your new best friend. SMART stands for Specific, Measurable, Achievable, Relevant, and Time-bound. It's a formula that helps transform vague aspirations into clear, actionable paths. For instance, instead of saying, "I want to save money," which is as undefined as saying, "I want to be famous," a SMART financial goal would be, "I want to save $1,000 for a laptop by saving $100 every month for the next ten months." This goal isn't a dream; it's a plan.

Specific and Measurable are about knowing what you're aiming for and how you'll know when you've hit your target. Achievable is the reality check because, let's face it, saving a million dollars by next Tuesday isn't happening. Relevant ensures the goal matters to you because you're far more likely to pursue a goal that has personal significance. Lastly, being time-bound means setting a deadline, which helps keep the procrastination gremlins at bay.

The Benefits of Vision Boards

Let's get creative with a vision board, which isn't an arts and crafts project—it's a powerful tool to keep your financial aspirations front and center. A vision board is a physical or digital collage of images, quotes, and items representing your financial goals. Seeing a picture of that dream car, the island vacation, or the sleek new laptop can serve as frequent motivation. Place it somewhere you'll see it daily, like your bedroom wall or as a background on your phone. Every time you see it, you're reminded of where you want your financial journey to take you, keeping the motivation fresh.

While dreaming big is vital (who doesn't want to reach for the stars?), there's a pragmatic side to goal-setting that requires bridging the gap between dreams and reality. It's fun to imagine being a billionaire by 25, but setting such an unrealistic goal can lead to frustration and financial burnout. The trick is to aim high but start small. Maybe you aspire to buy a house. Break it down: Start by saving for a down payment. Convert your dreams into smaller milestones that lead you step by step toward that larger goal.

Tracking progress is like having checkpoints in a marathon. It helps you know how far you've come and how far you must go. Regularly reviewing your financial goals is crucial because life isn't static. Maybe you get a raise (yay!), or unexpected expenses pop up (not so yay). Adjusting your plans ensures you stay on track rather than veering into the financial wilderness. Tools like budgeting apps or simple spreadsheets can help monitor your progress. Set a monthly or quarterly review as a recurring event in your calendar, making these check-ins a regular part of your financial routine.

Remember, the point of setting financial goals isn't just to achieve them—it's to live the life you want. Money is a tool in that process, and mastering its management starts with setting goals as real as they are inspiring. So, dream big, plan smart, and keep those financial targets in clear view.

CHAPTER 2
BUDGETING BASICS

Picture this: You've landed your first gig, or maybe you've pocketed sweet cash from lawn mowing or babysitting. There's a thrill that comes with seeing those dollars stack up, right? But then comes the part where those same dollars vanish by the end of the month. Where does it all go? If figuring that out feels like trying to solve a mystery, then welcome to the world of budgeting—a skill not exclusively for the old and boring but for anyone who wants to boss up their financial game.

2.1 CRAFTING YOUR FIRST BUDGET: A STEP-BY-STEP GUIDE FOR TEENS

Understanding Income and Expenses

Let's break down what budget is: it's a plan for your money. Simple, right? The first step in crafting this plan is to figure out what you're working with, which means understanding your income and expenses. Start by tallying how much money you bring in each month. That could be your part-time job, weekly allowances, or side hustles. Get the total figure, and that's your income.

Next, track where your money is going. Categorize your spendings like food, entertainment, transportation, or that sneaky category often forgotten—miscellaneous. Jot down what you spend daily for a month. Yes, that $4 coffee counts. By the end of the month, you'll have a clear picture of where your cash is flowing, often revealing surprising facts about your spending habits.

The 50/30/20 Rule

Let's simplify budgeting with a nifty guideline known as the 50/30/20 rule:

1. 50% of your income should go to 'needs' — essentials like food, rent, and transportation.
2. 30% goes to 'wants' — this is the fun part, where you spend on things like movies, games, or that trendy pair of shoes.
3. 20% is set aside for savings or paying off debts.

This rule is a solid framework to start with because it's flexible to fit different incomes and lifestyles. Adjust the percentages, if necessary, but it gives you a clear blueprint for allocating your funds effectively.

Budgeting for Irregular Income

If your income looks more like a rollercoaster than a steady climb due to part-time gigs or freelance jobs, budgeting feels like fitting a square peg in a round hole. Try calculating your average monthly income based on the past few months. Use this average to set your monthly budget. During months when you earn more, resist the temptation to splurge. Instead, boost your savings. When you earn less, you'll have that cushion to lean on without breaking your budget. Keep yourself busy. The busier you are, the less time you have to look for unnecessary items.

Tools and Methods

Gone are the days of budgeting with only pen and paper, although it's still a solid option. Today, the digital world offers plenty of tools that make budgeting simpler, faster, and more fun. Apps and online tools automatically track your spending, categorize expenses, and send alerts when you hit the spending limit in any category. Compare a few tools to find one that suits your style—

some enjoy the simplicity of a spreadsheet, while others prefer an app that visually breaks down their spending habits with colorful charts and graphs.

Interactive Element: Budgeting Quiz

Ready to test your budgeting knowledge? Dive into this quick quiz to see if you've got the basics down and discover areas to focus on more.

Outgrow - Budgeting Quiz

Crafting your first budget might feel daunting, but think of it as the first step toward financial freedom. It's about making your money work for you, not the other way around. By understanding your income and expenses, using the 50/30/20 rule as a guide, adjusting for irregular income, and leveraging modern tools, you're on your way to becoming a budgeting pro. So, grab your financial reins and start planning — your future self will thank you!

2.2 APPS AND TOOLS TO MAKE BUDGETING EASIER AND FUN

Managing your finances with pen and paper feels like using a map instead of GPS. It works, sure, but why not simplify the process with some tech flair? The digital age has blessed us with an array of apps and tools designed to make budgeting not just more accessible but kind of fun. Imagine that—fun budgeting!

Fun Budgeting Apps

Let's explore some apps that are both user-friendly and effective. Think of these apps as your financial assistants—they keep track of your spending, help you set goals, and provide insights on where you can cut back without feeling like you're on a financial diet. Apps like Mint and YNAB (You Need A Budget) are stellar at this. They sync with your bank accounts and categorize your spending automatically. No more guessing how much you spent on coffee last month—the numbers are clear as day.

Mint   YNAB   Rocket Money

The app I started with, which is now called Rocket Money, is an amazing app paying as low as $4 a month with similar functionality as the others. That is one cup of coffee from Starbucks a month.

Gamification

Onto making budgeting engaging through gamification. Yes, budgeting can be as engaging as your favorite video game. Apps like Fortune City take a unique approach by turning your financial activities into a city-building game. Every transaction you record helps you build and upgrade your virtual city. It's like playing SimCity or Stardew Valley, but your crops and buildings are real-life budget entries.

With great power (or great apps, in this case) comes great responsibility. Let's talk about security. While it's awesome to have these powerful tools at your fingertips, protecting your personal information is paramount. Always check the security features of any budgeting app before diving in. Look for apps that use encryption to protect data transfers, offer two-factor authentication for an extra layer of security, and have clear privacy policies that ensure they're not selling your data to third parties. A good budgeting app protects both your money and your privacy.

Integrating these tools into your daily life is daunting, but it's about creating habits. Setting regular check-ins with your budgeting app can make all the difference. Maybe you spend 15 minutes reviewing your budget every Sunday night and preparing for the week ahead. Make this a ritual—play music, eat a snack, and dive into your financial summary. Over time, this check-in won't be a habit; it'll be a part of your life that you look forward to.

2.3 AVOIDING COMMON BUDGETING PITFALLS FOR YOUNG ADULTS

You've started your budgeting journey, armed with apps and strategies, and you're feeling good, right? Hold up a minute. Even the best financial warriors stumble into classic budgeting traps. Let's navigate these pitfalls together so you can dodge them.

The Different Saving Approaches

First up, the classic overestimation game. It's easy to fall into the trap of overestimating how much money you'll have each month. Maybe you think, "Hey, I'll definitely make more tips next week," or "I'm sure I'll sell more crafts online." Optimism is a great trait, but when it comes to budgeting, it can lead to spending money you don't have. This is where brutal honesty with yourself about your income comes in. Track what you earn, not what you wish to earn. Use the lower end of your average income to plan your budget. This way, you're not caught off-guard and don't find yourself diving into the savings you don't have.

Next, let's discuss the 'out of sight, out of mind' approach to savings. Many fall into the trap of treating savings as an afterthought—a nice-to-have once all the spending is done. Flip that script and make savings a non-negotiable part of your budget. Think of it as paying your future self. Set up an auto-transfer to your savings account right on payday. The money is saved before you spend it, making savings a built-in part of your financial plan, not just leftovers you scrape together at the end of the month.

Now, about those sneaky, small expenses—I'm looking at you, gourmet coffee and weekend online movie rentals. These little purchases seem harmless, but they add up, nibbling away at your budget like a mouse in a cheese factory.

Start tracking every dollar. You'll be surprised how much you spend on these 'treats.' Setting a weekly limit for these expenses helps keep your budget on track without feeling deprived.

Lastly, a rigid budget is like a stiff pair of new jeans—it doesn't leave much room to breathe. Life is unpredictable. Your car breaks down, you get a surprise invitation to a friend's destination wedding, or you get a sudden opportunity to take an extra class that advances your career. If your budget is too rigid, these unexpected expenses can throw it into chaos. Build flexibility into your budget by setting aside a small 'just in case' fund for unforeseen expenses. This flexibility can help you handle life's curveballs without busting your budget.

Budgeting is about more than restricting where your money goes. It's about creating a clear path for your money that aligns with your life. By avoiding these common pitfalls—overestimating income, forgetting about savings, ignoring small expenses, and lacking flexibility—you can create a budget that not only works today but also adapts to tomorrow's changes.

As we wrap up this chapter on the essentials of budgeting, remember the goal here isn't just to keep your finances in check but to empower you to make informed financial decisions that propel you toward your dreams. You've learned how to create a budget and confirm it's robust, responsive, and realistic. The future chapters will build on this foundation, diving deeper into how you enhance your savings strategies and invest your wealth. Keep this budgeting wisdom close, and let's keep pushing forward.

CHAPTER 3
EARNING AND MANAGING INCOME

I magine this: you've landed your first real job, and you're about to receive your first paycheck. You're picturing a fat stack of cash—maybe you want a new gadget, a cool pair of sneakers, or a concert ticket. But when you tear open that envelope or check your bank account, the number seems... smaller than expected. Welcome to the world of deductions, taxes, and the sometimes-baffling difference between gross and net income.

Don't sweat it! This chapter is here to empower you, transforming you from a paycheck rookie to a savvy income manager. If you have received a paycheck, you know what deductions are, but you might not understand them. Stick around to learn and understand more about how they work.

3.1 NAVIGATING YOUR FIRST JOB: UNDERSTANDING YOUR PAYCHECK

Deciphering Your Paycheck

First things first, let's break down that paycheck stub. It might look like a jumble of numbers and confusing terms, but each piece of information has its significance. Typically, your paycheck will show your gross income, which is your total earnings before any deductions. Then come the deductions—these can include federal and state taxes, Social Security, Medicare, possibly a retirement contribution, and maybe health insurance premiums. What you're left with after these deductions is your net income, or what you get to take home. Understanding these deductions is not just a theoretical exercise; it's crucial to your financial well-being.

For example, federal and state taxes are withheld based on the information you provide on your W-4 form. It's like a mini quiz on how much tax you think should be taken based on your financial situation. Getting this right can mean not owing a scary amount at tax time or not letting the government hold onto too much of your money throughout the year. Social Security and Medicare, often shown as FICA on your stub, are contributions that build up your entitlement to receive benefits in the future. If you see a deduction for a 401(k) or another retirement plan, that's your future self thanking you for making your life a bit easier down the road.

Please watch this 1 minute video on understanding your pay stub

Budgeting with Net Income

Let's talk budgeting with your net income. Budgeting with your net income helps keep your financial feet on the ground, preventing you from overspending and facing a bank account that screams 'surprise!' at the end of the month. Start by tracking your net income for a few months to establish a realistic view of your monthly earnings, which can fluctuate, especially if you're in a job with variable hours or commissions.

Negotiating Your Salary

Nothing spikes the heartbeat like sitting across from your boss trying to prove your worth in monetary terms. But here's the thing: learning to negotiate your salary or a raise is a powerful skill that impacts your financial health. Start by researching what your role typically pays in your industry and region (websites like Glassdoor and PayScale are great for this). Arm yourself with this information, along with a list of your achievements and responsibilities that go beyond your basic duties. Approach the negotiation as a conversation about your value. The worst they can say is no, but they could also say yes—which will never happen if you don't ask.

Benefits and Perks

Benefits and perks can add significant value to your job satisfaction and financial well-being. They're not simply 'extras ', but part of the overall package that makes up your compensation. Health insurance, life insurance, and retirement plans like a 401(k) with employer match are worth their weight in gold.

There are less apparent perks like tuition reimbursement, flexible working conditions, or wellness programs that can save you money. Evaluating and utilizing these benefits can enhance your overall financial landscape.

3.2 SIDE HUSTLES: TURNING PASSIONS INTO PROFITS

Ever thought about turning your weekend photography gigs or your knack for baking into a steady stream of extra cash? Welcome to the world of side hustles, where your passions can bring you joy and potentially pad your wallet. It's like hitting two birds with one stone, but instead of birds, we're talking about fun and finances. Let's dive into how you can transform what you love doing into a profitable side hustle and, more importantly, how to juggle this with your studies or a full-time job without burning the candle at both ends. Here is a list of Side hustles you can look into

Online and Remote Work

1. **Freelance Writing**: Writing articles, blog posts, or copy for websites.
2. **Graphic Design**: Creating logos, business cards, and marketing materials.
3. **Web Development**: Building and maintaining websites.
4. **Virtual Assistant**: Providing administrative support to businesses or individuals.
5. **Online Tutoring**: Teaching subjects or skills online.
6. **Social Media Management**: Managing social media accounts for businesses or influencers.
7. **Content Creation**: Producing videos, podcasts, or blogs for online platforms.

8. **Transcription Services:** Converting audio files into text.
9. **Online Surveys:** Participating in surveys for market research.
10. **E-commerce:** Selling products on platforms like Etsy, eBay, or Amazon.

In-Person Services

1. **Ridesharing:** Driving for services like Uber or Lyft.
2. **Food Delivery:** Delivering food for companies like DoorDash or Uber Eats.
3. **Handyman Services:** Offering repairs and maintenance services.
4. **Pet Sitting/Dog Walking:** Caring for pets while owners are away.
5. **House Cleaning:** Providing cleaning services to homes or offices.
6. **Event Planning:** Coordinating and planning events or parties.
7. **Photography:** Offering photography services for events or portraits.
8. **Personal Training:** Providing fitness training and coaching.
9. **Tutoring:** Teaching subjects in person.
10. **Childcare/Babysitting:** Looking after children.

Creative and Hobby-Based

1. **Craft Selling:** Making and selling crafts or handmade goods.
2. **Music Lessons:** Teaching musical instruments or vocal skills.

3. **Art Commissions**: Creating custom artwork for clients.
4. **Writing a Book**: Publishing your own book, either traditionally or self-published.
5. **Gardening/Landscaping**: Offering gardening or landscaping services.

Technology and Digital

1. **App Development**: Creating and selling mobile apps.
2. **Software Testing**: Testing software applications for bugs.
3. **SEO Services**: Providing search engine optimization for websites.
4. **Affiliate Marketing**: Promoting products and earning a commission on sales.
5. **Domain Flipping**: Buying and selling domain names for profit.

Investments and Finance

1. **Stock Trading**: Buying and selling stocks or other securities.
2. **Cryptocurrency**: Investing in or trading cryptocurrencies.
3. **Real Estate**: Renting out properties or flipping houses.
4. **Peer-to-Peer Lending**: Lending money through online platforms for interest.

Miscellaneous

1. **Mystery Shopping**: Evaluating customer service for companies.
2. **Renting Out Space**: Renting out a room or property on Airbnb.

3. **Task-Based Platforms:** Completing tasks on platforms like TaskRabbit.
4. **Test Websites/Apps:** Providing feedback on user experience.
5. **Voiceover Work:** Recording voiceovers for commercials or videos.
6. **Car Advertising:** Placing ads on your car for a fee.

Seasonal/Occasional

1. **Holiday Decorator:** Setting up holiday decorations.
2. **Event Staffing:** Working at events or festivals.
3. **Seasonal Retail:** Working in retail during peak seasons.

Local Services

1. **Moving Services:** Helping people move their belongings.
2. **Lawn Care:** Offering lawn mowing or landscaping services.
3. **Snow Removal:** Clearing snow during winter.
4. **Errand Services:** Running errands for busy individuals.

Skill-Based

1. **Language Translation:** Translating documents or conversations.
2. **Consulting:** Providing expert advice in your field.
3. **DIY Projects:** Building and selling custom furniture or decor items.

Identifying Skills and Passions

The first step in turning your hobby into a money-making venture is identifying which skills or passions can become profitable. Ask yourself: What do I love doing that others might pay for? Maybe it's graphic design, fitness training, or tutoring. Once you pinpoint your passion, it's time to validate its market demand. A simple way to test this is by starting small—offer your services or products to family and friends or through local online forums.

Now comes the nitty-gritty part: monetizing your hobby. This stage involves setting up a basic business model. How will you charge? Per hour, per project, or a flat rate? For instance, if you're into photography, you can start by offering portrait sessions at a flat rate.

Next up is branding. Create a catchy name and logo that reflects your hustle's spirit and set up social media profiles or a simple website to showcase your work and attract clients. Do not spend money creating a logo when you are starting. There are websites where you can make a beautiful, eye-catching logo for free. Type in Google "Free logo designs," and try different websites until you find the logo fit for you and your work. You can also use apps like Logopit Plus for logos.

The next step is to create Facebook and Instagram pages, post pictures of your product or service, and follow as many local people as possible. The people getting the request might follow you or like your business page. The more jobs you do, the more reviews you get. Everyone takes some time to pick up entrepreneurship but do not let time discourage you from having a successful side hustle. This digital presence acts as your portfolio as well as your marketing hub.

Balancing Side Hustles with Life

Balancing a side hustle with your regular commitments can be the trickiest part. It's like playing a game of Tetris with your time. Allocate specific hours each week to your side hustle, assuring it doesn't overlap or interfere with your studies or job. Use tools like calendars or planner apps to keep track of your commitments. More importantly, listen to your body and mind. If you're feeling overwhelmed, it might be time to scale back. Remember, it's essential to maintain a healthy balance to avoid burnout.

Navigating the Legal Side

Navigating the legal and tax implications is another critical aspect. Depending on where you live, turning a hobby into a business might require registering it, especially if your earnings exceed a certain threshold. That could mean registering for a business license and possibly paying taxes on your income.

Keeping a record of all your transactions, expenses, and income is essential. It might be worth consulting with a tax professional to ensure you're on the right side of the law and to help you discover any deductions you could claim.

Creating Entities

Do not create an entity right off the bat. In my example, I made a vending machine business entity, but my sales and clientele were low, and I had to file taxes and a bunch of documentation I didn't know about. Don't put yourself through that until you have a business that sells at least 20-30k a year.

You will hear everywhere about how you should create an entity to file tax deductions, but how much can you tax deduct from a business selling 10k a year? Barely anything. It will be more paperwork that stresses you out.

When doing an entity, research, talk to people who own businesses, and watch YouTube videos on how they did it. You are not alone; people want to help. Here are some videos to help you understand the different types of entities and how to open an LLC. Note, creating an LLC may vary depending on your state, but the video will help you get a good idea of where to start.

Explaining different types of Entities

How to Create an LLC

Be mindful that every state and county is different. Inform yourself how to open a business and file taxes in your state. Also, do not hire a CPA (Certified Public Accountant) to do your bookkeeping until your sales are over 50k a year or have employees on W2. Use websites like QuickBooks—this will also be a money saver. I recommend doing yearly taxes with a CPA. More than likely you will do something wrong if you tried to do them yourself.

Scaling Your Side Hustle

Scaling your side hustle into a more substantial business venture is an exciting prospect. It means your little project is growing up! That doesn't have to happen overnight. Monitor the growth, demand, and your capacity to handle increased work. Scaling might involve outsourcing tasks, such as accounting or marketing, to focus more on what you do best. It could also mean expanding your product line or services to reach a broader audience.

Success stories of teens turning their passions into profit are inspiring and instructive. Take Zoe, a high school student who started making custom illustrations for her friends. She posted her creations on socials, and soon enough, commissions rolled in. She expanded her client base by using word of mouth and leveraging Instagram as her portfolio, balancing schoolwork and growing business.

Or consider Liam, who turned his passion for coding into a freelance app development service, eventually partnering with local businesses to create customized apps. These stories highlight that your side hustle can soar with the right blend of passion, planning, and perseverance.

As you look to convert your free-time fun into a revenue stream, remember that starting small, staying organized, and being mindful of legalities will set a solid foundation for your venture. Whether it's extra pocket money or the beginnings of a career, the world of side hustles holds endless possibilities.

3.3 FREELANCING 101: MANAGING IRREGULAR INCOME

When you decide to dive into the freelancing pool, the freedom of choosing your clients and projects is exhilarating. However, that freedom comes with the unpredictability of not knowing when your next paycheck will arrive or how much it will be. Managing finances with an irregular income can feel like trying to build a sandcastle one moment and then watching the tide wash it away the next. With some innovative strategies, you can make your financial sandcastle sturdy enough to withstand the waves.

How to Start Freelancing

The key here is to create a buffer—a financial cushion that helps you smooth out the peaks and valleys. Start by calculating your average monthly income over the last six months to a year. This average will give you a baseline to work with for your budget. Next, prioritize your essential expenses like rent, utilities, and groceries. Whatever is left can be allocated to your wants and savings. Speaking of savings, funnel a portion of your income into an emergency fund. This fund is your lifeline when work slows or unexpected expenses pop up. Aim to build a buffer that covers at least three to six months of living expenses.

Finding freelance gigs can sometimes feel like searching for a needle in a haystack. However, the digital age has made connecting with potential clients more accessible. Online platforms like Upwork, Freelancer, and Fiverr are reliable. These platforms allow you to showcase your portfolio, set your rates, and apply for projects that match your skills.

Another powerful tool in your arsenal is networking. Connect with other freelancers and industry professionals on LinkedIn or in relevant online forums. Attend workshops and seminars in your field to meet potential clients and learn from established freelancers. Every person you meet could know someone who needs your skills, so don't be shy about sharing what you do.

Setting Rates and Contracts

Setting your rates and getting paid are critical aspects of your freelancing career. Research what others in your field are charging by checking out freelance forums or industry pricing guides. Set competitive rates that reflect your skills, experience, and the complexity of the projects you take on. Always clarify payment terms before starting a project. Will you be paid per hour, per project, or at milestones throughout the project? Use invoicing software to bill your clients and keep track of payments. Consider asking for a deposit upfront, especially for larger projects, to ensure you're not left high and dry if a client backs out.

Contracts are not only formalities but your safeguard in the freelancing world. A well-drafted contract should outline the scope of the project, deadlines, revisions, payment terms, and what happens if the contract is terminated early. This clarity protects you and the client by guaranteeing everyone is on the same page. Don't be afraid to negotiate terms. If a client's proposed rate is too low, counter with a rate that better matches your value. Be professional and assertive—your skills are worth it. The right clients will recognize and respect that.

Navigating the freelance landscape requires creativity, discipline, and financial savvy. By setting up a solid financial buffer, actively seeking out opportunities, setting fair but competitive rates, and securing your work with contracts, you can turn your freelance endeavor from a side hustle into a thriving business. As you grow your skills and expand your network, you'll find that freelancing can offer income and a fulfilling way to work on your terms.

3.4 PROTECTING YOURSELF AGAINST FRAUD AND SCAMS

The digital world is a playground not just for memes and TikToks but also for some not-so-fun stuff like scams and frauds. It's like walking through a neighborhood that has pickpockets lurking around. Whether you're paying your bills online or selling your custom graphic tees, understanding how to spot these digital pickpockets and protect your hard-earned cash is crucial.

Scammers have gotten crafty, but their tricks have common red flags. For instance, phishing emails or messages look like they're from legit companies asking you to update your account or confirm some personal details. They might stress urgency, like "Act now, or your account will be closed!" But here's the scoop: real businesses won't ask for sensitive information via email or text.

Another popular scam targeting young folks is the promise of easy money, which might come in the form of a "too-good-to-be-true" investment opportunity or a part-time job with unbelievable pay. Remember the golden rule: if it seems too good to be true, it probably is. Always double-check the source before clicking on any links or sharing your info, and when in doubt, reach out directly to the organization through official channels.

Strong passwords are your first line of defense. Think of them like the lock on your front door. You wouldn't want it to be something obvious that anyone could guess, right? Use a mix of letters, numbers, and symbols, and avoid common words or easy sequences like "password123." Even better, use a password manager to keep track of your more complex passwords. It's like having a digital keychain that's much harder to steal. Add an extra layer of security with two-factor authentication (2FA). It's like a double-lock system where, even if someone gets your password, they still need a second code (usually sent to your phone) to get in.

Getting Scammed

What if, despite your best efforts, you get scammed? First, don't beat yourself up about it. It can happen to anyone, and it's not a reflection of your intelligence or savvy—it's just that some scammers are good at what they do. Here's what you can do: Act fast. If you suspect you've been scammed, immediately contact your bank or credit card company to report the fraud and protect your accounts. Then, report the scam to the relevant authorities. That might include your local consumer protection agency or a national fraud reporting center. They might not always be able to get your money back, but they can take action to prevent the scammer from hurting others.

Lastly, let's chat about financial privacy. In an age where sharing is part of life, it's easy to share too much. Oversharing personal information online can lead to identity theft, where a scammer uses your details to open accounts in your name or guess your security questions to access your accounts. Keep your personal information, like your home address, phone number, and especially your Social Security number, off social media and other public platforms. Treat your personal information like you would an embarrassing secret; share it sparingly and only with people you trust.

We've covered how to recognize scams, protect yourself with solid practices, and what steps to take if you find yourself a victim of a scam. As we move forward, remember each step you take builds toward your financial resilience. Up next, we'll delve into savings strategies that will protect and enhance your financial landscape.

CHAPTER 4
SAVINGS STRATEGIES

L et's shift gears and talk about something that might make your future self want to travel back in time to high-five you —saving money. I know what you're thinking: "Saving money? But isn't that something my grandparents are obsessed with, alongside their antique coin collections?" Well, yes, but here's the secret— they're onto something.

Saving isn't just about stashing cash for the gray hair days; it's about giving yourself the power to make choices and take chances, whether that's starting a business, traveling the world, or buying that dream setup for your gaming adventures. One of the most powerful tools in your savings arsenal is compound interest, which can turn your small savings into a significant nest egg over time.

4.1 THE POWER OF COMPOUND INTEREST: START SAVING NOW

The Magic of Compounding

Let's start with what might seem like a magic trick but is just math —compound interest. Imagine you plant an apple seed. This seed grows into a tree and produces more seeds, then grows into more trees. Over time, you don't have one tree; you have an orchard. That's compound interest in the world of savings. Your money grows not exclusively from your initial deposit but also from the interest that accumulates over time. The sooner you start, the more "trees" you can grow.

Compound interest works because the interest you earn each year is added to your original balance. That earns more interest the following year, and so on. It's interest on interest, which grows your savings over time. Simply put, it's like adding magic dust to your savings, turning something small into something surprisingly big.

Early Starts Lead to Big Soaring Returns

Starting early can be the difference between a small grove and a vast forest. Let's say you start saving $100 a month at age 20, with an interest rate of 5% compounded annually. By the time you hit 30, you won't have the $12,000 you saved; you'll have around $15,528. Start at 30; by 40, you'll have about $14,487. Notice the difference? Thanks to our friend compound interest, that extra decade can boost your savings. The earlier you start, the more time your money has to grow and the more you'll have.

How to Open Your First Savings Account

Opening a savings account is like setting up a new realm for your money to grow safely. First, shop around. Look at different banks and financial institutions and compare their savings account options. Look at the interest rates, fees, and minimum balance requirements. Online banks often offer higher interest rates than traditional brick-and-mortar banks because they have lower over-head costs. Once you choose, you'll typically need some ID, your Social Security number, and an initial deposit to open your account. It's a simple process that can be done online in a few minutes.

Compound Interest Calculators

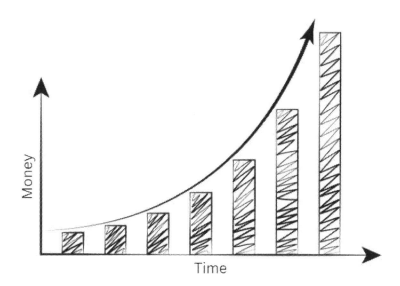

To see the potential growth of your savings, check out a compound interest calculator. These handy tools let you experiment with different scenarios and see how your money could increase. By changing the variables, like the amount you plan to save each month or the interest rate, you can see how minor adjustments can make a massive difference in the long run. Websites like Investor.gov present free calculators to help you visualize your savings growth and plan better for your future.

4.2 CREATIVE SAVING HACKS FOR THE YOUNG AND RESTLESS

Let's face it, saving money feels like a chore, but what if I told you there are hacks out there that can make saving as exciting as spending? Yes, you heard that right. Let's dive into some creative ways to save that won't make you yawn or think about your grand-parents' penny-pinching era.

Round-up Savings Apps

Round-up savings apps are like the digital equivalent of throwing your loose change into a piggy bank, but instead, it's your digital transactions that are doing the saving. Apps like Acorns or Chime offer features where your purchases round to the nearest dollar, and the difference transfers into a savings or investment account. Every time you buy a latte, music download, or bus ticket, you're saving without trying. It's stealthy saving, and it adds up. You could save a few hundred dollars a year without any painful sacri-fices. It's like finding money in your winter jacket from last season —a pleasant surprise that boosts your savings.

Challenge Savings Plans

For those who enjoy a challenge and love seeing direct results, challenge savings plans can add some spice to your savings routine. Ever heard of the 52-week money challenge? It's simple yet effective. You save $1 in the first week, $2 in the second, $3 in the third, and so on. By the end of the year, you'll have tucked away a neat $1,378! Not too shabby, right? You can reverse the challenge by starting with $52 in the first week and going backward, which could be easier if you're worried about holiday season expenses. The best part? You can tweak the challenge to match your budget. If $1 increments are too steep, try 50 cents. What starts as a fun challenge could become a solid savings buffer by year's end.

Utilizing Cashback and Rewards

Moving on to something a little more instantly gratifying cashback and rewards. You can earn rewards or cashback on your everyday purchases with the right credit cards or apps. But here's the key—you must be smart about it. Look for cards or apps that offer rewards on the stuff you already buy. If you're a foodie, look for a card that gives extra points at restaurants; if you're always on the move, how about cashback on gas? Services like Rakuten offer cashback for shopping at a wide range of online retailers, which can be a game-changer if you're already buying online. Just remember, this isn't an excuse to spend more. Instead, it's about making your regular spending work harder for you. And when you get that cashback, funnel it straight into your savings. It's like making your money do double duty.

Social Savings

Saving money can be more motivating—and a lot more fun—when you bring friends or family into the mix. Whether challenging a friend to a savings duel or starting a savings club, where each member contributes a small amount each month, pooling resources can lead to big rewards. You can set collective goals, like saving up for a group vacation, or help each other reach personal goals, offering support and accountability. Apps like Splitwise can make managing shared expenses easier, ensuring everyone stays on track without any awkward money conversations. Your next adventure could be funded not solely by you but by a collective effort of your closest buddies.

4.3 SETTING UP YOUR EMERGENCY FUND: HOW MUCH IS ENOUGH?

Let's chat about something that might not be as thrilling as your latest TikTok binge, but trust me, it's every bit as crucial—setting up an emergency fund. Think of it as your financial safety net, designed to catch you if you stumble. Whether it's an unexpected car repair, a sudden medical bill, or the classic case of 'I lost my job,' an emergency fund guarantees you don't spiral into a financial frenzy.

The Importance of an Emergency Fund

The role of an emergency fund can't be overstated. It's the buffer that keeps your financial ship steady in stormy seas. Without it, you might be tempted to swipe your credit card, diving deeper into debt, or worse, you might be forced to skimp on essentials. With a solid emergency fund, you stand on firmer ground.

Calculating Your Emergency Fund

While one-size-fits-all might work for some accessories, it doesn't apply here. A good rule of thumb is to have enough to cover three to six months of living expenses. That includes your rent, food, utilities, and other monthly necessities. Add up must-pays, then multiply by the number of months you want to cover. This total is your target emergency fund.

Strategies to Build It Fast

Don't worry, there are strategies to help you grow this fund without feeling like you're pinching pennies till they scream. Consider setting up an automatic transfer to your emergency fund right after payday—think of it as paying your future self first. Even a small amount, like $50 monthly, starts adding up. You can also look for ways to boost your income temporarily. Maybe pick up freelance gigs, sell items you no longer need, or consider a temporary part-time job. Every extra dollar can be funneled into your emergency fund, speeding up its growth.

Maintaining and Managing Your Emergency Fund

Once your emergency fund is set up, keeping it intact is challenging. It can be tempting to dip into it for that unplanned tech upgrade or a last-minute concert ticket. To resist the temptation, keep your emergency fund in a separate savings account—one that's not too easy to access but available when you truly need it. Online savings accounts are a good option. They offer better interest rates and can be a tad less accessible than your main bank account, keeping the temptation at bay. Regularly review your emergency fund. As your expenses increase or decrease, or as your life circumstances change, so should the size of your emergency fund.

This fund isn't about restricting your financial freedom but enhancing it. It's about ensuring that when life does happen, you're ready, financially speaking. So, take these steps, build that fund, and sleep a little easier knowing you have a safety net.

Remember the key points: the transformative power of saving early, the creative ways to make saving engaging, and the critical role of an emergency fund. Each strategy is a step toward not only financial security but financial empowerment. Next up, we'll dive into the exciting world of investing. It's one thing to save your money, but learning how to make it grow? That's where things get interesting.

CHAPTER 5

INVESTING FOR BEGINNERS

You've been acing the saving game, so let's explore the world of investing, where your money can work for you 24/7, even while you're enjoying your favorite show or studying. Investing is a realm of possibilities where your money can grow, multiply, and dance to the rhythm of the markets.

5.1 STOCKS, BONDS, AND MUTUAL FUNDS: AN INTRODUCTION

Basic Investment Types

Think of the investment world as a buffet. You've got several dishes to choose from—stocks, bonds, and mutual funds, each with its own flavor and level of spice.

First up: Stocks. Buying stock is like buying a tiny piece of a company, like buying a slice of your favorite pizza. If the company does well, the value of your stock can go up, and you might get a bonus slice (that's money the company pays you for holding onto its stocks). But if the company doesn't do well, the value of your stock may drop. Stocks are like the roller coasters of the investment park—high potential rewards but with some stomach-churning drops.

Next: Bonds. Imagine lending money to a company or government. In return, they promise to repay with interest after a certain period. Bonds are like the Ferris wheels of the investment world—slower, steadier, and a safer bet. They may not offer as high returns as stocks, but they provide security and stability.

Lastly: Mutual funds. These are like those fancy tour buses that take you to several sightseeing spots. When you invest in a mutual fund, you're pooling your money with other investors, and a professional manager is choosing a mix of stocks, bonds, and other assets to invest in. It's a solid way to get a diversified portfolio without picking each investment yourself. Here is a video that helped me get my feet wet on how to read stock charts.

Benefits of Mutual Funds

For beginners, mutual funds are like having a GPS while traveling in a new city. They present professional management, which means you have an experienced fund manager making investment decisions on your behalf. This manager works to ensure the fund's portfolio is well-positioned to achieve its goals, whether that's growth, income, or stability. Plus, because mutual funds invest in ranges, they promote built-in diversification, which can help manage risk.

How the Stock Market Works

Speaking of investments, let's demystify how the stock market works. Think of it as a giant, bustling marketplace where pieces of companies (stocks) are bought and sold. Prices change based on supply and demand, like how concert tickets get pricier when a band is super popular. The stock market is influenced by everything from economic indicators and company earnings to global events and investor sentiment. It's a dynamic environment, always moving and shaking.

Diversification

One golden rule in investing is diversification. It's like not putting all your eggs in one basket. Instead of betting everything on one stock or bond, you spread your investments across various types to reduce risk. If one investment has a bad day (or year), others might do well and balance things out. Mutual funds are perfect for achieving diversification because they invest in a broad range of assets, spreading out potential risks and opportunities.

Investment Terminology

Before we go any further, let's swipe through some essential investment terms you'll want to get cozy with:

1. Portfolio: Your collection of investments.
2. Asset Allocation: How you divide your investments between different types (like stocks, bonds, and cash).
3. Volatility: How much the value of an investment goes up or down.
4. Yield: The income returned on an investment, like the interest received from a bond.

Understanding these terms will help you navigate investment discussions and make informed decisions.

Choosing Investments

Start by defining what you're investing for. Are you planning for long-term goals like retirement or shorter-term goals like buying a car or saving for a trip? Your timeframe will influence your investment strategy. For long-term goals, you might consider stocks. For shorter-term goals, bonds or more conservative mutual funds might be a better fit. Remember, you're in control of your investment journey, and there's a strategy that suits your needs.

There's no one-size-fits-all answer to investing. It's about what works for you. Think about your risk tolerance—are you okay with risky swings in your investment value if it means a higher return potential? Or does the thought make you queasy? Be honest and choose investments that fit your comfort level and financial objectives.

Investing isn't just for the Wall Street wizards—it's for anyone who wants to see their money grow. With the proper knowledge and strategies, you're on your way to making informed, confident investment choices that help you reach your financial dreams.

5.2 YOUR FIRST INVESTMENT ACCOUNT: GETTING STARTED

Are you ready to take the plunge and open your first investment account? That's like deciding to learn to drive—exciting, a bit nerve-wracking, but a step toward new horizons. Picking where to park your money (and watch it grow) is your first decision, and it's an important one. Think of investment platforms as different types of cars. Some are flashy and fast, with all the latest tech, while others are more reliable and user-friendly. The key is choosing a brokerage or investment app suitable for your style and goals.

When selecting a platform, consider three main factors: fees, features, and user experience. Fees can eat into your returns like termites, so search for platforms with low or no commission fees on trades. Some may charge monthly fees but offer free trade, while others may provide more services like automatic rebalancing or tax-loss harvesting.

Features are your tools—does the platform have educational resources? What about customer support? Is there mobile access? Make sure it has the features that support your learning and investing style. A platform with an intuitive interface can make your investment journey smoother and less intimidating.

Opening an Account

It's less paperwork than you fear. You'll need personal information —your name, address, Social Security number, employment information, and financial situation. Most platforms ask you to set up a way to fund your account, like linking a bank account. You'll also need to decide on the type of investment account. Are you opening a standard taxable account or looking into retirement options like an IRA?

Start small with your first investment. Decide how much you're comfortable with investing. Many platforms allow you to start with tiny amounts, even providing fractional shares of stocks, meaning you can buy a piece of a company without needing to pay for a full share. It's an effective way to start without committing much money.

Understanding fees is imperative because they can sneak up on you. Look beyond the trading fees. Check for annual fees, inactivity fees, or fees related to withdrawals or transfers. Every dollar you pay in fees is a dollar not growing through investments. If you're unsure, don't hesitate to ask their customer support.

Lastly, here's a quick word on taxes because Uncle Sam wants a piece of your gains. Investments are subject to different forms of taxation. For example, dividends (your share of a company's profits) and capital gains (the profit you earn from selling your investments at a higher price than you paid) are taxable. The rate varies based on how long you've held the investment. Short-term capital gains (for investments held less than a year) are typically taxed at higher rates than long-term gains. Keeping track of these details can help you manage your tax bill effectively. It might sound complicated, but don't worry—many platforms offer tools to help track this, and there's always professional help. Here is a QR code that helps you explain how the taxes work on stocks.

Setting up your first investment account is a big step that sets you on the path to financial growth and learning. By choosing the right platform, understanding the steps to get started, making informed investment choices, and being aware of fees and taxes, you're laying down the tracks for a successful investment adventure. Every investor starts somewhere!

5.3 NAVIGATING RISKS AND RETURNS: A BEGINNER'S GUIDE

When you step into the world of investing, it's like setting out on a road trip. You've got your map (investment goals), your vehicle (investment choices), and you're ready to hit the road. But like any good road trip, you need to understand the weather conditions (market risks) and have a solid idea of the balance between the speed (returns) and safety (risks) you're comfortable with.

Risk and Return

Generally, investments with higher potential returns come with higher risks. Stocks, for example, have attractive growth opportunities but can also be volatile. Bonds, on the other hand, usually have lower returns but less risk compared to stocks. Balancing these risks and returns is critical. It involves aligning your investment choices with your financial goals and how much risk you can stomach. If you're saving for a long-term goal, like retirement, you might lean toward investments with higher growth potential, accepting the short-term ups and downs. However, if you're saving for a short-term goal, such as a down payment on a house, you might prioritize lower-risk investments to ensure the money is there.

Evaluating investment opportunities is another critical skill. Fundamental and technical analysis are two navigational tools at your disposal. Fundamental analysis involves looking under the hood of potential investments—examining company financials, market conditions, and economic indicators to assess a stock's intrinsic value. It's like checking your car's engine and tires before a long trip. Technical analysis focuses on statistical trends from trading activity, such as past prices and volume. Both methods can provide valuable insights, helping you make informed decisions about where to invest your money.

Beginner Mistakes

One major mistake is emotional investing, where decisions are driven by feelings rather than facts. That can lead to impulsive moves, like selling stocks during a market dip due to fear or buying into a 'hot tip' without proper research.

Another frequent error is trying to time the market to predict its highs and lows to make quick gains. That is as risky as trying to beat a speeding train at a crossing—it might work once, but it's dangerous and unsustainable. Avoid these pitfalls by sticking to your investment plan and focusing on long-term goals rather than short-term fluctuations.

Lastly, embracing the principles of long-term investing can smoothen your investment journey. This approach is about patience, consistency, and the power of compounding returns— the financial equivalent of compound interest, where your investment earnings generate their own earnings over time.

By investing regularly, reinvesting profits, and staying invested through market ups and downs, you harness the potential of the market's long-term growth trend.

Navigating the twists and turns of investing can be challenging, but with a clear understanding of the risks and returns, a solid strategy for evaluating opportunities, and a commitment to avoiding common mistakes, you're well-equipped to manage your investment portfolio effectively.

5.4 NAVIGATING CRYPTOCURRENCY: A BEGINNER'S PERSPECTIVE

Let's dive into the buzzing world of cryptocurrency, which might feel like the Wild West of the investment landscape, but hold your horses! Before you saddle up and ride into this frontier, it's important to understand what you're getting into. Cryptocurrency, or crypto for short, is like virtual money. Imagine if instead of carrying cash or cards, your money was digital. That's what cryptocurrencies like Bitcoin, Ethereum, and others are.

Cryptocurrencies are built on something called blockchain technology. Think of it as a super sophisticated ledger that records all transactions transparently and securely. Unlike traditional currencies issued by governments (known as fiat currency), crypto operates independently of a central authority. This independence can be appealing because it suggests a kind of financial freedom from typical bank controls and government interventions. However, it also means there's no safety net, which is why diving into crypto requires understanding both the shiny potential and the significant risks. Below are some logos of Crypto that you may recognized.

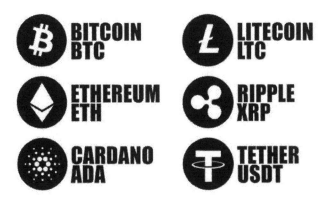

Risks and Rewards

Early investors in cryptocurrencies have made fortunes as the value of these digital assets has skyrocketed at various points. Plus, the technology behind cryptocurrencies—blockchain—is groundbreaking and could revolutionize everything from finance to contracts to how we vote. But here's the flip side: crypto markets are incredibly volatile. Prices can swing wildly in short periods, making it possible to see both dramatic gains and painful losses within a day. This volatility is because the crypto market is new. There's also the risk of regulatory changes as governments figure out how to deal with these digital assets.

Getting Started Safely

If you're set on testing the waters, start by dipping a toe—don't dive headfirst. Understand what you're buying and why. Are you interested in technology, the potential for profit, or following a trend?

Once you decide to invest, use a reputable exchange. Think of exchanges like cryptocurrency shops where you can buy, sell, or trade your digital currencies. Platforms like Coinbase, Binance, and Kraken have built reputations for being user-friendly and relatively secure.

When it comes to storing your cryptocurrency, you have digital wallets. These wallets can be online, on your desktop, or even on a hardware device (like a USB stick but for crypto). Each type has its balance of accessibility and security. Online wallets are convenient but more vulnerable to hacking. Hardware wallets, while less convenient, provide a fortress for your digital coins. Always remember to keep your passwords and keys secure. Losing them might mean losing your crypto forever, with no bank to call to get it back.

Long-Term Perspective

While the thrill of quick profits is tempting, adopting a long-term perspective is wiser. Cryptocurrency is still in its infancy, and the market is speculative. Prices go up based on investor enthusiasm rather than actual value, which leads to bubbles and crashes. If you decide to invest, consider it part of a diversified investment portfolio. That means not putting all your eggs in the crypto basket. Think of crypto as a spice in your investment stew—not the main ingredient.

Viewing cryptocurrency as a long-term investment also means preparing to ride out volatility. It's about looking beyond daily or even monthly fluctuations and focusing on what the value might be in years to come. This approach requires patience, a level head, and an acceptance of being in for a bumpy but potentially rewarding ride.

The key to successful investing lies in education, careful planning, and a clear understanding of your financial goals and risk tolerance. Up next, we'll explore advanced saving and investing strategies that can help you further enhance your financial toolkit.

CHAPTER 6
ADVANCED SAVING AND INVESTING STRATEGIES

I magine you're playing your favorite video game and unlock a secret level—a shortcut that allows you to skip ahead and gain extra powers or resources. What if I told you that starting your retirement savings as a teen is like unlocking a secret level in real life? It's not just a powerful move; it's a move that puts you in control, propelling you ahead in the game of financial security. Let's dive into how you can start building that financial super-power today.

6.1 RETIREMENT SAVING FOR TEENS: WHY START NOW?

Compounding Interest: The Magic Multiplier

Think of compounding interest as your financial BFF, who's good at cloning money. Here's the scoop: every dollar you save gets you the initial amount back and earns more dollars over time. And then those new dollars earn more, and so on. For example, if you start saving $50 a month at age 15, with an average annual return of 7%, by the time you hit 65, you wouldn't have saved just $30,000. Thanks to compounding, that initial amount could grow to over $200,000!

That's like turning a small investment into a down payment for a house or a college fund for your future children. The kicker? The earlier you start, the more your money grows without you having to lift a finger (or another dollar). It's like planting a tree that grows money leaves—the sooner you plant it, the bigger and leafier it gets.

Types of Retirement Accounts: Choose Your Financial Container

Retirement accounts have different powers and drawbacks. For teens, a Roth IRA is like a hero choice. Why? The money you put in comes from after-tax income, meaning you've already paid taxes. So, when you withdraw it at retirement, you don't owe Uncle Sam a penny more, not even on the earnings! It's remarkable because, unlike traditional IRAs, Roth IRAs let you withdraw your contributions (but not the earnings) anytime without penalties. This flexibility is your safety net, great for young investors who need access to their money for significant life events, like college or buying a first home.

Contributing to Retirement Accounts: Every Little Bit Counts

You might think, "But I'm just a teen. I don't have much money to contribute!" That is a fair point, but remember, small amounts can become considerable sums over time thanks to our pal, compounding interest.

Start with what you can. It could be money from a summer job, a part-time gig, birthday cash, etc. Many Roth IRAs have low minimum contribution requirements, some as little as $25. Setting up automatic contributions can also keep you consistent. Think of it as a subscription to your future self that pays off big time.

We will cover more about Roth IRAs and their benefits in chapter 10.

Long-Term Financial Health: Building Your Economic Immunity

Like how eating well and exercising can build your physical health over time, starting your retirement savings early builds your financial health. It's about more than stashing cash for old age; it's about creating a buffer against life's uncertainties—economic downturns, job losses, or unexpected expenses.

Early savers are more likely to develop disciplined spending habits, better credit scores, and a deeper understanding of financial planning. All these contribute to a robust economic foundation, giving you the freedom to choose based on what you want in life, not only what you need. Start now and envision the financial freedom and stability you can achieve.

Interactive Element: Compound Interest Calculator

Want to see how your savings could grow? Check out this compound interest calculator.

This tool allows you to experiment with different scenarios and see the potential growth of your savings. You can plug in various amounts, interest rates, and times to see how small, regular contributions balloon into significant sums.

Play around with it—what happens if you skip a coffee a week and save that money instead? Prepare to be amazed by the power of early and consistent saving!

6.2 BUILDING WEALTH WITH REINVESTING AND COMPOUND INTEREST

Power of Reinvesting Earnings: Speeding Up the Growth

Let's amp up that magic by reinvesting your earnings, which means taking the interest you earn and putting it back into your investment. Reinvesting supercharges the compound interest effect. Each time you reinvest your profits, you increase the base amount based on your interest calculations. It's as if every dollar of interest you earn starts working for you, earning interest.

Picture this: if you continue to reinvest the interest you earn from that initial $1,000 investment at 5%, you're making money from your original $1,000 and the additional interest earned each year. Over 20 years, that initial $1,000 investment could grow to over $2,650 without you having to add any more money from your pocket. It's like your money clones itself, and those clones go to work and start cloning themselves, too!

Here is a QR code to a compound that is highly recommended. (invest at your own risk)

Practical Examples: Seeing Compound Interest in Action

To see the real power of compound interest, let's look at two friends, Jamie and Taylor, who decide to invest. Jamie starts putting $100 a month into a retirement account with an annual interest rate of 5% at age 25. Taylor does the same but waits until age 35 to begin. By the time they reach 65, Jamie has contributed $48,000, and Taylor has contributed $36,000. However, because of the extra ten years of compounding, Jamie's investment has grown to about $162,000, while Taylor's has grown to about $83,000. Jamie almost doubled the total, not because she invested a lot more but because she gave her investments more time to develop.

Starting Early: Why Sooner is Way Better

Imagine you start a garden in the spring and enjoy an entire season of growth. Or you can wait until fall and try to cram all your gardening into the few weeks before winter hits. Starting to save and invest early gives your money the entire season to grow, thrive, and multiply. It's about giving your wealth the maximum amount of time possible to benefit from each cycle, making the task of building substantial wealth less about how much you invest and more about how long you let it grow.

6.3 EXPLORING REAL ESTATE INVESTING ON A SMALL SCALE

When you think about investing in real estate, you might picture some high-flying mogul buying up skyscrapers or swanky beachfront properties. But here's the secret: you don't need to be a millionaire to start investing in real estate. In fact, there are several strategies that make real estate accessible even if you're starting out and your bank account isn't overflowing. Let's unpack some of these options and see how you can get your slice of the real estate pie.

Exploring REITs

Real Estate Investment Trusts (REITs) are like the appetizers of the real estate world—they give you a taste without requiring buying the meal. REITs are companies that own or finance income-producing real estate across a range of sectors. They work a bit like stocks and are traded on major exchanges. By investing in a REIT, you're buying a piece of a portfolio of real estate assets, which could include malls, hospitals, offices, or apartments. This means you can earn dividends from real estate without having to buy, manage, or finance any properties yourself. It's a hands-off approach that can still offer the benefits of real estate investment, like regular income and appreciation potential.

Crowdfunding

Crowdfunding platforms are another exciting option, especially for those who want to dip their toes into real estate but need more time to dive in. These platforms allow you to join other investors to fund a project, whether it's developing a new building or renovating an existing one.

Each investor contributes a small amount of money toward the total needed, and in return, you get a share of the profits if the project succeeds. It's like crowdfunding a cool new gadget, but instead, you're helping to fund real estate projects. This method allows you to be more selective with your investments and choose projects aligning with your interests and financial goals.

The Unpredictable Market

As much as real estate investing sounds like a thrilling ride, it's not without its bumps. The market can be unpredictable, and properties can take a significant amount of time and money to develop or sell. Plus, unlike stocks, real estate is not a liquid asset; it can't be quickly and easily sold for cash without potentially incurring a loss. However, with careful planning and smart strategies, these risks can be managed.

For instance, diversifying your real estate investments can protect you from downturns in any single market. Also, thorough research into properties and markets can help you find investments with the best potential returns. Always consider factors like location, market trends, and economic forecasts since they impact real estate value.

How To Start Real Estate

First, educate yourself. Read books, listen to podcasts, or take courses on real estate investing. Understanding the basics will help you make informed decisions and navigate the complexities of the real estate market.

Next, set clear financial goals. Are you looking for quick profits through property flipping, or are you more interested in long-term income through rental properties? Your goals will guide your strategy and help you decide where and how to invest.

Finally, start small. Your first investment doesn't have to be a multi-million-dollar deal. Consider starting with a small REIT investment or joining a low-cost crowdfunding project. As you gain experience and confidence, you can gradually scale up your investments.

Why Choose Real Estate

Real estate investing offers a tangible way to grow your wealth, and thanks to modern investment options like REITs and crowd-funding, it's more accessible than ever. By understanding the benefits and risks, starting small, and being smart about your investments, you can build a promising real estate portfolio. This approach diversifies your investment strategy and adds a solid layer of security to your financial future.

Like any form of investing, real estate requires patience, research, and a clear understanding of your financial goals. With these tools in hand, you're well on your way to becoming a savvy real estate investor.

Keep in mind the powerful role that early and informed investment decisions can play in building your financial security. Whether it's maximizing the benefits of compound interest, exploring the potential of retirement accounts, or stepping into the world of real estate, each strategy offers unique advantages and challenges.

Let's continue to expand our financial knowledge and skills by diving into the intricacies of credit and debt management.

CHAPTER 7
BUILDING WEALTH

Have you ever imagined yourself as a millionaire before you turn 30? It might seem like a far-fetched dream, but here's a secret—it's within your reach. Building wealth isn't just for the privileged or the exceptionally talented. With the right strategies, a bit of discipline, and a touch of smartness, you can create a financial empire or at least a respectable kingdom. Ready to learn how? Let's get started.

7.1 THE PATH TO BECOMING A MILLIONAIRE BY 30

Leveraging High-Growth Investments: The Wealth Accelerators

To supercharge your wealth-building journey, you'll need more than a savings account. Enter high-growth investments like stocks and real estate. These are your wealth accelerators, potentially offering higher returns compared to your run-of-the-mill savings accounts or bonds. Yes, they come with higher risks, but remember, with great risk often comes great reward.

As mentioned before, diversifying your portfolio across different asset classes can help manage these risks. Think of it as an investment smoothie—blending stocks, bonds, and real estate to create a balanced, nutritional mix that suits your financial palate and growth goals.

Entrepreneurship as a Wealth-Building Strategy: Your Business Empire

If you're feeling particularly adventurous and have a knack for innovation, entrepreneurship could be your golden ticket to wealth building. Starting your own business can be an exhilarating path to financial freedom, allowing you to capitalize on your passions and potentially reap substantial rewards. But, like any daring adventure, it comes with its share of challenges like financial risk, market competition, and the sheer grind of getting a business off the ground.

The key here is resilience and adaptability. Learn from each setback, pivot your strategies as needed, and keep your eyes on the prize. Remember, many of the world's most successful entrepreneurs started with little more than a dream and determination.

Mindset and Habits of Millionaires: The Millionaire's Playbook

Ever wonder what sets millionaires apart? It's not just their bank accounts but their habits and mindsets. Embracing frugality doesn't mean skimping on all life's joys; it means valuing and maximizing resources.

Lifelong learning keeps you on top of financial trends and strategies, sharpening your investment acumen. Perseverance, the backbone of any success story, ensures you stay on course. Integrating these habits can transform your finances and approach to life.

Visual Element: The Millionaire's Mindset Pie Chart

Imagine a pie chart sliced into sections labeled 'Economizing', 'Continuous Learning', 'Investment Savvy', and 'Perseverance'. The slices represent a core component of a millionaire's mindset. This chart not only serves as a fun visual but also as a constant reminder of the balanced approach needed to reach your financial goals.

By embracing early and consistent investing, leveraging high-growth opportunities, exploring entrepreneurship, and adopting the mindset of millionaires, you're not just dreaming of wealth—you're building it. Remember, the path to becoming a millionaire by 30 isn't reserved for the lucky few; it's accessible to anyone willing to learn the ropes and put in the work. So why not you?

7.2 PASSIVE INCOME IDEAS FOR EARLY WEALTH BUILDING

Let's chat about passive income, a term that conjures images of earning money while lounging on a beach somewhere exotic. But before you pack your sunscreen, let's break down what passive income is and why it's a game-changer in wealth building.

Simply put, passive income is money you earn with minimal to no ongoing effort. It's like setting a clever machine on your desk that cranks out dollars while you go about your life. Sounds sweet, right? Well, it's a critical component of building wealth because it can provide financial security and freedom, diversifying your income streams beyond the traditional 9-to-5 job.

Generating Passive Income

Let's dive into one of the most popular ways to generate passive income as mentioned earlier: real estate investment. There are several strategies tailored to different levels of investment and involvement. For instance, rental properties can be a fantastic source of steady monthly income. Whether it's renting out an entire apartment or a room on Airbnb, being a landlord can pad your wallet. Of course, it requires some upfront investment and ongoing management, but with the right property in a desirable location, the rental checks can become a reliable income stream.

Applying REITs

I joined REITs in 2023, and it's opened my eyes to a new way of real estate investing. Elaborating from the last chapter, these are companies that own or finance income-producing real estate. By investing in a REIT, you're buying shares in a portfolio of properties, ranging from apartment complexes to shopping malls, without the hassle of managing them. Most REITs are traded on major stock exchanges, and they're required by law to pay out at least 90% of their taxable income to shareholders in the form of dividends. This makes them a great source of passive income, and because they're traded like stocks, you can buy or sell shares quickly if your financial goals or circumstances change.

Dividends

Shifting gears from real estate to the stock market, dividends are another excellent way to earn passive income. When you own dividend stocks, you receive a portion of the company's earnings periodically. It's like being a silent partner in a business where you reap the rewards without participating in the day-to-day operations. To streamline this process, consider investing in dividend index funds. These funds are collections of stocks known for issuing high dividends, managed professionally, which spreads out your risk and simplifies your investment strategy. Some of the best dividend annual yield companies are CMCSA, BMY, MO, MPC, FANG, and VICI. As always, research as their yearly dividend yield could change among other companies.

The Digital Frontier

Lastly, let's talk about the digital frontier: creating and selling digital products. This could be anything from an eBook about your backpacking adventures to a course on web design. Once you create and set up these products for sale, they can continuously generate income without much additional effort. The beauty of digital products lies in their scalability. You create something once, and it can be sold over and over to anyone, anywhere in the world, without needing to restock inventory or handle shipping. Plus, platforms like Amazon for eBooks or Udemy for courses make it easier than ever to reach potential buyers.

Building passive income streams allows you to take control of your financial future by creating ongoing earnings that don't require trading your time for money. Whether it's through real estate, dividends, or digital products, the key is to choose avenues that fit your interests and financial situation. By setting up these income streams, you're not just working for money—you're making money work for you. Why not start exploring these options? Your future self will look back and thank you for making such smart, forward-thinking financial decisions.

7.3 FINANCIAL INDEPENDENCE, RETIRE EARLY (FIRE): IS IT POSSIBLE FOR YOU?

Imagine living a life where you're not tied down by a nine-to-five job, and your days are yours to enjoy as you please. That's the dream, right? Well, it's not just a pipe dream. It's what the FIRE (Financial Independence, Retire Early) movement is all about.

Explaining FIRE

The core principle of FIRE revolves around a few key strategies: extreme savings, aggressive investing, and minimizing expenses. Think of it as turning all the traditional financial advice you've heard up to eleven. Instead of saving 10% of your income, what if you saved 30%, 40%, or even 50%? It sounds intense, but that's the level of commitment we're talking about. Every dollar saved is a step closer to buying your freedom from mandatory work.

Aggressive investing goes hand in hand with extreme saving. The money you save isn't sitting in a jar; it's working hard in the markets. That might mean investing in stocks, bonds, mutual funds, or real estate—assets that can grow your wealth over time.

The idea is to turn your savings into a robust investment portfolio that generates enough returns to cover your living expenses without you needing to work.

Calculating Your FIRE Score

Calculating your FIRE number is the next step. This is the amount you need to have in your investment pot to safely withdraw enough to cover your expenses year after year. A common rule of thumb used in the FIRE community is the 25x rule, which suggests you need 25 times your annual expenses saved up. So, if you spend $40,000 a year, you're aiming for $1 million. To figure out your number, track your spending to understand how much you need annually, then multiply that by 25.

However, the FIRE journey is not all about money—it's also about lifestyle choices and sacrifices. It requires you to live differently from many of your peers, often spending less and saving more. It might mean skipping the latest iPhone release, cutting back on eating out, and opting for less expensive vacations. These sacrifices can be challenging, especially if you feel like you're missing out. However, for many, the trade-off is worth it. The key is to decide what's important to you. This decision is deeply personal and requires honest self-reflection.

Retirement Through FIRE

Navigating the path to financial independence and early retirement through the FIRE movement can be incredibly rewarding, but it's not without its challenges. It requires a high level of financial discipline, a willingness to make massive lifestyle changes, and a commitment to long-term goals. Yet, for those who've walked this path successfully, the rewards—both financial and personal—are immense.

As we wrap up, remember that whether this path is right for you, understanding these principles can enrich your financial literacy and empower you to make informed decisions about your money and your life.

Share Your Financial Freedom Journey!

Don't forget to use #FinancialFreedomJourney on social media and share your successes with the world. There's another way you can inspire more people like you to take this empowering journey as well – you can leave a review online.

Simply by sharing your honest opinion of this book and a little about your own journey so far, you'll inspire new readers to equip themselves with all the knowledge they need to set off on the road to financial freedom.

Thank you so much for your support. I can't wait to hear about your successes!

Scan QR code to leave review

CHAPTER 8
CREDIT AND DEBT MANAGEMENT

I magine you're at an amusement park called Financial Freedom Land. You're excited, map in hand, ready to explore all it has to offer. Suddenly, you see it: the Credit Score Rollercoaster. It might not look as thrilling as the Debt Dodge Cars or the Investment Rocket, but oh boy, strap in! Understanding and managing this ride is vital to exploring the rest of the park smoothly.

8.1 CREDIT SCORES UNVEILED: WHAT THEY ARE AND WHY THEY MATTER

Basics of Credit Scores

First up, what is a credit score? Think of it as a financial report card that grades you on how well you handle your money and debts. Ranging from 300 to 850, this number is calculated based on several factors: your payment history, amounts owed, length of credit history, new credit, and types of credit used. The higher your score, the better you look to potential lenders, landlords, and sometimes even employers. Why? Because a high score signals that you're good at managing debts responsibly, which means less risk for them.

Improving Your Credit Score

How can you boost this number? Here are some actionable steps:

1. Pay your bills on time, every time. This is the single most important factor in your credit score. Set reminders, use auto-pay features, and do whatever it takes to ensure you never miss a payment.
2. Keep your credit card balances low. High outstanding debt can negatively affect your score. Try to use no more than 40% of your credit debt. What I always do is only use 10% of my credit card balance, using it consistently and paying off every month.
3. Hold onto old credit cards. Older accounts boost your credit history, assuming they're in good standing.

4. Limit new credit applications. Each time you apply for credit, it can cause a slight dip in your score. So, apply only when necessary.
5. Diversify your credit. A mix of credit types—credit cards, auto loans, Mortgage loans—can sometimes help your score.

Impact of Credit Scores on Financial Opportunities

Having a solid credit score opens a world of opportunities. For starters, it can mean lower interest rates on loans and credit cards, which translates into thousands of dollars saved over time. Planning to buy a car or a house? A good score can make these goals more attainable and affordable. Even landlords check credit scores to decide if you're likely to be a reliable tenant. In other words, a good score saves you money and broadens your financial options.

Common Credit Score Myths

Let's clear up some myths:

1. Myth: Checking your credit score will hurt it. False. Checking your own score is a "soft inquiry" and doesn't affect it. Only "hard inquiries," like when a lender checks your score, can impact it.
2. Myth: You need to carry a credit card balance to build credit. Nope. Paying off your balance in full each month demonstrates your good management skills and keeps you debt-free.

3. Myth: Your income affects your credit score. Income isn't directly factored into your credit score. However, lenders may consider it alongside your score to assess your ability to repay loans.

Interactive Element: Credit Score Improvement Checklist

To help you improve your credit score, here's a handy checklist:

1. Set up payment reminders for all your bills.
2. Pay down balances on credit cards, starting with the highest interest rates.
3. Review your credit report for errors and dispute any inaccuracies.
4. Avoid opening new lines of credit unnecessarily.
5. Regularly monitor your credit score to track your progress.

Remember, improving your credit score is like training for a marathon—it takes time, consistency, and patience, but the rewards are worth the effort.

8.2 THE DOS AND DON'TS OF USING CREDIT CARDS

Exploring the realm of credit cards feels like being in a candy store —everything looks inviting, but not everything is good for you. Credit cards help you build a solid credit score, snag those sweet cashback deals, and manage cash flows smoother than a hot knife through butter. But mishandle them and they're more like opening a Pandora's box that could take years to shut. Let's guarantee we're using this tool for all its perks without falling into the traps.

Responsible Credit Card Use

The beauty of credit cards isn't just in postponing payments or buying those concert tickets before payday. When used correctly, they're excellent for building your credit history—essential when you want to get a loan for a new car or get a mortgage for your first house. Each time you swipe responsibly and pay back on time, you're telling future lenders, "Hey, I've got this!" Plus, the rewards —oh, the rewards! From flight miles for your next adventure to cashback on groceries, it's like getting a mini 'thank you' note from your bank each time you spend.

However, the key is disciplined spending. Treat your credit card like your debit card: if you don't have the money in your bank account, think twice before buying. Always aim to pay off the entire balance each month. This avoids interest charges and builds your credit score. And about those rewards? Always check if the benefits outweigh the costs. Some cards come with hefty annual fees or high interest rates that might not be worth the rewards unless you're a big spender.

Avoiding Common Pitfalls

Let's talk about the pitfalls because, let's be honest, they're lurking around the corner. The most common misstep? The minimum payment trap. Paying only the minimum each month might seem like easing your financial burden, but it's more like a slow sink into quicksand. The remaining balance doesn't just sit there; it accumulates interest—often at rates that would make a loan shark blush. Before you know it, what was a manageable amount can balloon into a financial nightmare.

Another pitfall is the temptation to own multiple cards. More cards mean more potential rewards, right? Maybe, but they also mean more paperwork, more terms and conditions to keep track of, and more chances of missing a payment. If you decide to juggle several cards, keep a meticulous schedule of when each bill is due, and consider using financial management apps that alert you to upcoming payments.

Choosing the Right Credit Card

Selecting the right credit card is like picking the right tool for a job —it needs to fit your financial situation and goals. Start by assessing why you need the card: Is it for building credit, earning rewards, or perhaps for business expenses? Different cards cater to various needs. For building credit, consider cards that report to all three major credit bureaus. If rewards are your game, look for cards that offer the best returns on the types of spending you do most.

Also, consider the card's fee structure. If you like traveling abroad, a card without foreign transaction fees is worth its weight in gold. Always read the fine print—interest rates, penalty fees, and the reward program's specifics can all impact your wallet. Websites that compare credit cards can be handy here, letting you line up your options side by side to make a well-informed choice.

Credit Card Security

In an era where buying lunch can involve swiping a card, security is paramount. Always keep a watchful eye on your credit card activity. Most banks provide real-time alerts via SMS or email if they detect unusual activity—opt into these notifications. For online purchases, consider using virtual card numbers if your issuer provides them. These are temporary numbers that link to your account, so your actual card details remain hidden from merchants.

Protecting your physical card is just as crucial. A damaged card is a hassle, but a lost or stolen one is a disaster. If your card goes missing, report it immediately. Many issuers have a zero-liability policy for fraudulent transactions, but this is often contingent on you reporting the loss promptly.

By mastering the art of using credit cards effectively, you're managing money and enhancing your financial flexibility and security. Remember, a credit card is an economic tool, and like all tools, its value comes from how well you use it. So, use it wisely, stay alert to the pitfalls, and make your credit card a key player in your financial arsenal.

8.3 STRATEGIES FOR TACKLING STUDENT LOANS AND DEBT

Student loans—the sidekick you didn't ask for but ended up with on your adventure through college. Whether you're considering taking out loans or watching them pile up like unread messages, understanding the ins and outs can make a huge difference in how you manage and conquer them. Student loans aren't merely a common rite of passage; they shape your financial landscape for years post-graduation. So, let's break down the basics and some clever strategies to handle them without letting them handle you.

Understanding Student Loans

Student loans come in various states, each with its unique set of rules. First, federal loans are backed by the government and typically have lower interest rates and more flexible repayment options than their private counterparts. These include Direct Subsidized Loans (where the government pays the interest while you're in school) and Direct Unsubsidized Loans (where you're on the hook for the interest, which accumulates even while you're hitting the books). Then, private loans are sourced from banks, credit unions, and other financial institutions. While these can fill the gaps in college funding, they often come with higher interest rates and fewer relief options.

Choosing the right type of loan is like picking gear for a trek—the better suited it is to your situation, the less likely it is to weigh you down. Consider factors like interest rates, the flexibility of repayment plans, and the lender's reputation. Always exhaust federal loan options before turning to private loans; the former often come with safety nets like income-driven repayment plans, which adjust your monthly payments based on your income.

Repayment Strategies

Once you're out of college, the grace period ends, and it's time to start paying back. You'll have several repayment plan options, ranging from the standard ten-year plan to extended or income-driven plans. Picking the right plan feels like choosing a path in a maze—each has pros and cons, but the goal is to find one that aligns with your financial capacity and long-term goals.

For those aiming to minimize interest costs and clear the debt quickly, the standard plan is straightforward and painless if your budget allows it. However, if your entry-level salary makes frugal living seem like reckless spending, consider an income-driven repayment plan. These plans adjust your monthly dues to a percentage of your discretionary income, which can provide much-needed breathing room while you climb the career ladder.

Debt Avalanche vs. Debt Snowball Methods

Now, for the tactical part, how do you tackle multiple loans? The debt avalanche and debt snowball methods are popular strategies that help clear the deck faster. The avalanche method involves paying off the loans with the highest interest rates first. On the other hand, the snowball method focuses on paying off the smallest debts first, gaining momentum and motivation as each one is cleared. It's about celebrating small victories that empower you to take on more significant challenges.

Choosing between these methods depends on what motivates you more: saving money on interest or the psychological wins of paying off debts. Both strategies require discipline and a solid budgeting plan, but the sense of achievement with each cleared loan is worth the effort.

Seeking Forgiveness and Assistance Programs

If you're in public service, a teacher, or facing unique financial hardships, loan forgiveness programs are a light at the end of the tunnel. Programs like Public Service Loan Forgiveness (PSLF) can erase remaining debt after ten years of qualifying payments if you work in government, non-profit, or other qualifying positions. There are also forgiveness options for teachers and those in other service-oriented professions. Additionally, if you're struggling due to economic hardship or unemployment, deferment and forbearance options provide temporary relief by pausing your payments.

Dealing with student loans is undeniably complex, but with a clear understanding of your options and strategic planning, you can manage them effectively. Whether it's choosing the right type of loan, selecting a repayment plan that fits your budget, or utilizing strategies like the avalanche or snowball methods, the keys to conquering your student debt are within reach. And remember, exploring forgiveness and assistance programs gives further relief, helping you move toward financial freedom. So, take a deep breath, arm yourself with knowledge, and prepare to tackle your student loans with confidence.

8.4 STRATEGIES TO AVOID AND MANAGE DEBT

Debt: it's like that clingy friend from high school who keeps popping up just when you thought you were on a clear path forward. Managing it isn't only about making payments on time—it's about crafting a master plan that keeps you ahead of the game. Let's start with creating a solid debt repayment plan. Think of it as your personal roadmap out of Debtville.

Gathering Details

First, gather all the details of your debts: amounts, interest rates, and due dates. It's like assembling the pieces of a puzzle. Then, prioritize them—typically, you'd tackle high-interest debts first since they're the peskiest, growing faster than a neglected lawn. But, if small victories keep you motivated, you can start with the smallest debts to clear them off your list.

Debt Battle Plan

It's time to set up a battle plan. How much can you pay each month without living on instant noodles? This is where budgeting plays a superhero role. By understanding your cash flow, you can identify how much money you can divert toward debt without sacrificing your basic needs. Now, automate these payments. Like setting an alarm for your favorite TV show, automating assures you never miss a payment and keeps your credit score from dropping.

Using Debt Wisely

Yes, there's a smart way to handle debt! Not all debts are villains in your financial story. For example, a mortgage can be a stepping stone to owning a home, and student loans can be an investment in your education and future earning potential. The key is strategic borrowing. Before taking on debt, ask yourself: Will this debt bring me closer to my financial goals? Does it have favorable terms? Is the interest manageable? If it's a yes, this debt can be a tool, not a burden. Always have a clear repayment plan, and confirm the debt aligns with your long-term financial aspirations.

Debt Management

Lastly, let's arm you with resources for debt management. Knowledge is power, after all. Websites like the National Foundation for Credit Counseling (NFCC) have tools and counseling to help manage debt. Apps like Mint or YNAB (You Need A Budget) track your spending and plan for debt repayment. Don't overlook books on personal finance—many give time-tested advice on getting out of debt and managing your finances effectively.

With a clear repayment plan, a robust emergency fund, wise usage of debt, and helpful resources, you can manage and even leverage debt to your advantage.

In the next chapter, we'll explore planning for the future, where we'll discuss long-term financial goals and how to prepare for the financial milestones you'll encounter down the road.

More than Money

"A formal education will make you a living; self-education will make you a fortune."

JIM ROHN

The reason I'm so concerned about financial literacy isn't really to do with money. Well, it is to an extent, but it's really more about everything that comes along with understanding how to manage it properly. Financial literacy is your key to freedom, independence, and peace of mind, and I can tell you that those are things I lacked when I started out in the adult world. It was tough, and I know all too well how debt and bad financial decisions can weigh on your mind and generally take away from your quality of life.

I say this not to scare you, but to empower you. When you know the risks of not knowing how to do something, it makes you so much more motivated and committed to learning it – which I already know you are, or you wouldn't have made it this far through the book! While we've taken this moment to pause and reflect on why this is so important, I'd like to ask you to take a moment to pass this knowledge on to more young people.

I know that sounds like a lot of work, but it's surprisingly easy. All it takes to help more people find this information is to spread the word – and you can do that simply by leaving a short review.

By leaving a review of this book on Amazon, you'll help new readers find this crucial information easily, and that's going to make a huge difference to their quality of life.

Financial literacy is something we should all be taught, yet rarely is it covered in schools... and that means we must work together to make sure it's widely accessible. Your involvement is vital.

Thank you so much for your support. You're making an incredible difference.

CHAPTER 9
PLANNING FOR THE FUTURE-IN THIS CHAPTER

W e'll delve into the importance of long-term financial goals beyond retirement, the role of insurance in managing financial risks, and the decision-making process between renting and buying a home. Imagine you're not just a passive viewer but the director of your financial movie. You're playing the lead role and deciding the plot. That is your story, and your long-term financial goals are the script. Whether studying to become an astronaut, owning a cozy cabin in the woods, or backpacking across Europe, each goal is a scene you'll eventually bring to life. But just dreaming about it isn't enough—like any good director, you need a solid plan to guarantee the end credits roll just the way you want. So, let's grab our director's chair and start shaping your financial blockbuster!

9.1 LONG-TERM FINANCIAL GOALS: MORE THAN JUST RETIREMENT

Identifying Life Milestones

Alright, so retirement feels a gazillion years away, but planning isn't just about stacking cash for your golden years—it's also about those big moments that make life, well, life. Think about what milestones you want to hit. Is it getting that master's degree? Buying your first home? Or maybe you dream of a wedding on a Hawaiian beach? Each of these goals has a price tag and a timeline. Start by jotting them down. Yes, right now! Grab a piece of paper or open a new note on your phone and list your dreams. This list is your roadmap, guiding you through the financial planning process.

Setting Actionable Goals

Let's turn these dreams into actionable goals by diving into what I mentioned before: SMART goals. We'll break it down by letter:

1. Specific: Get clear about what you want. "I want to buy a home" is a start, but "I want to buy a two-bedroom apartment in Austin in 12 months" is a screenplay waiting to be written.
2. Measurable: Attach numbers to your goals. How much will that apartment cost? Research current market prices to set a realistic target.
3. Achievable: Be honest with yourself. Is your goal doable in the time frame you've set, considering your current financial situation?

4. Relevant: Guarantee your goals align with your values and long-term vision. Does owning a home fit with your lifestyle, or would you rather have the flexibility to travel?
5. Time-bound: Set a deadline. Deadlines create urgency and can spur you into action.

Investment Strategies for Long-Term Goals

Investing can transform your financial goals from ideas to reality. However, not all investments are the same, and the best choice depends on how soon you need the money and how comfortable you are with taking risks. For instance, if you're planning to fund a master's program in five years, you might consider investing in things like bonds or fixed deposits that present stability. On the other hand, if you're saving for retirement, which is still a long way off, you might consider investing in stocks or mutual funds, which have the potential for higher returns despite their ups and downs.

Monitoring and Adjusting Goals

Your life isn't static, and neither should your financial plans be. Maybe you switch careers, move to a different city, or decide that owning a home isn't for you after all. That's totally fine! Regularly review your financial goals—at least once a year—to reflect any changes in your life and adjust your plans. It's like being a pilot; you need to check your coordinates and adjust your course to reach your destination.

Visual Element: Goal-Setting Flowchart

To help you visualize the process of setting and achieving long-term financial goals, here's a QR code to a flowchart. It starts with identifying your goals, followed by setting SMART criteria and choosing appropriate investment strategies, and ends with regular reviews to adjust goals as needed. This flowchart can be your visual guide, reminding you how to turn your financial dreams into reality.

By taking control of your financial narrative through careful planning, clear goal setting, strategic investing, and regular reviews, you're scripting a life of fulfilled dreams and achieved milestones. So, keep your director's hat on and your eyes on the prize; your future is waiting to be written!

9.2 UNDERSTANDING INSURANCE: TYPES YOU NEED EARLY ON

Think of insurance as your financial guardian angel. It's that friend who's got your back, stepping in to shield you from wallet-crushing disasters. Whether it's a fender bender on your way to a concert or a stolen laptop during finals week, insurance is there to help manage the risks that come with adulting.

Insurance, in plain speech, is a way to manage your risk. When you buy insurance, you're transferring the cost of a potential loss to the insurance company in exchange for a fee, known as a premium. In return, the insurance company promises to cover financial losses if certain bad things happen under the terms of your policy. Think about it like this: you're paying a little now to avoid paying a lot later. It's a cornerstone of sound financial planning because it helps protect you from financial losses that could derail everything from your savings goals to your future.

As a young adult, you're at a stage where certain types of insurance are essential. Let's break them down:

1. Health Insurance: This one's a no-brainer. Medical care in the U.S. can be staggeringly expensive, and a single accident or illness could set you back thousands if you're uncovered. Health insurance helps cover these costs and delivers preventive care that could catch issues before they become serious. Whether you're on your parent's plan, a student health plan, or shopping for your own policy through a marketplace, make sure you're covered.

2. Auto Insurance: If you drive, auto insurance is a must—not just because it's legally required in most places, but because it can help cover expenses if you're involved in an accident. Depending on your coverage, it helps pay for repairs, replacement costs, and even medical bills for you and your passengers.

3. Renters Insurance: Think you don't need insurance because you're renting and don't own the place? Think again. Renters insurance can protect your belongings if they're stolen or damaged by a covered risk, like fire or

vandalism. Plus, it's generally affordable. If someone gets hurt in your rented pad, it could help cover legal expenses if you're found liable.

4. Life Insurance: You might think life insurance is for old folks, but it can be a wise move for young adults, especially if you have dependents or debt. If something were to happen to you, a life insurance policy could help support those who depend on you financially. The younger you are when you get it, the cheaper it generally is.

Choosing the proper coverage levels and not overpaying for insurance is more art than science. Start by evaluating what you own and what kinds of financial risks you might face. How much would it cost to replace your laptop, bike, or guitar? What if you were in a car accident? Answering these questions can help you figure out how much coverage you need. Shop around, compare prices and terms, and read the fine print. Insurance policies can be dense, and the devil is often in the details—like what's covered.

Common terms you'll encounter include 'premium' (what you pay for the policy), 'deductible' (how much you pay out of pocket before insurance kicks in), 'coverage limits' (the maximum amount the insurance company will pay for a covered loss), and 'exclusions' (what's not covered). Understanding these terms can help you choose the best policy for your needs and avoid surprises when you file a claim.

The world of insurance isn't thrilling, but think of it as a crucial part of your financial toolkit. Just like you wouldn't go on a road trip without a spare tire, you shouldn't venture through life without the proper coverage.

9.3 REAL ESTATE BASICS: RENTING VS. BUYING YOUR FIRST HOME

So, you're thinking about your next big move—literally. The question of whether to rent or buy your first home is like deciding between two epic concert tickets. One might be right up your alley style-wise, but the other could be a better bang for your buck in the long run. Let's jam through the pros and cons of each to help you figure out which ticket to buy into the housing market.

Renting vs. Buying: What's Your Style?

Renting is like subscribing to Spotify: you pay each month to enjoy your tunes (aka your pad) without worrying about maintenance or long-term commitments. It's flexible. Did you get a job offer in another city? You can move without the hassle of selling a house. Plus, renting doesn't tie up your cash, so you can save or invest in other things. However, rent can be pricey and unpredictable. Rates may increase each year, and since you don't own the place, you're not building equity or getting tax benefits.

Buying, on the other hand, is more like buying your favorite vinyl record. It's yours to keep, personalize, and hopefully, it increases in value over time. Owning a home can offer stability, predictable payments (if you opt for a fixed-rate mortgage), and tax advantages. Not to mention the pride of ownership—painting walls neon green, no landlord can stop you! But it also comes with responsibilities like repairs, maintenance, and upfront costs such as down payments and closing fees. It's a more extensive initial playlist, but you could end up with a classic album that appreciates over time.

The Home Buying Process: From Dreaming to Owning

Thinking about buying? Here's a quick tour through the process. First up, get pre-approved for a mortgage. This is like the VIP pass at a concert—it shows sellers you're serious and ready to rock and roll. Next, find a real estate agent. Think of them as your band manager, someone who knows the ins and outs of the housing market and can lead you to your dream home.

Once you find a place that hits all the right notes, you make an offer. If it's accepted, you're on to the home inspection to guarantee everything is in tune with no hidden surprises like a faulty foundation or a roof on its last leg. If everything checks out, you close the deal, which involves lots of paperwork but ends with you getting the keys. Congratulations, you're now a homeowner!

Understanding Mortgages: The Financial Symphony

Mortgages seem complex, but they're loans for buying property. Think of them as your financial backing band. The most common type is a fixed-rate mortgage, providing a constant interest rate and monthly payments that never change. It's predictable, but there's also the adjustable-rate mortgage (ARM), which can change based on market conditions.

Key points include the interest rate, determining how much extra you'll pay to borrow the money, and the term, or how long you have to pay back the loan. Standard terms are 15 or 30 years. Shorter terms generally have higher monthly payments but lower overall interest, meaning you pay less over the life of the loan.

Renting Smart: Making the Most of Your Lease

If buying a home is more commitment than you're ready for, make sure you're a smart renter. Understand your lease agreement—it's the setlist for your rental experience. Know what your rent covers and what falls on your shoulders. Do you need to budget for utilities, or are they included? What about renter's insurance?

Manage your rental costs by staying on top of maintenance issues. A leaky faucet can lead to higher water bills. Also, be a good tenant. Paying rent on time and keeping the place in good shape makes it easier to negotiate with your landlord when it comes to renewing your lease or requesting repairs.

Researching the real estate market, whether renting or buying, is a significant step. By understanding the benefits and responsibilities of each option, you choose what aligns with your lifestyle and financial goals.

Next, we'll explore how understanding taxes secures financial freedom and growth. Get ready to decode tax jargon and discover strategies that could save you money and enhance your financial playlist.

CHAPTER 10
TAXES MADE SIMPLE

J ust hearing the word taxes might make you want to run for the hills but stick with me here. Imagine taxes are like a new app. At first, it seems complex and full of levels you might never understand. But once you start playing, you learn the rules, unlock tricks to score higher, and you're beating levels you thought were impossible. That's what we're about to do with taxes: break them down, understand the rules, and score some wins that leave more money in your pocket.

10.1 YOUR FIRST TAX RETURN: A STEP-BY-STEP GUIDE

Filing Basics

Filing a tax return for the first time can feel like you're trying to solve a puzzle with half the pieces missing, but don't worry, I've got you covered.

The first thing you need to know about filing your taxes is the deadline: April 15th of each year, unless it falls on a weekend or holiday, then it's the next business day. Missing this deadline is like showing up late to a concert–you might end up paying extra (in this case, in penalties).

You'll need key documents to file your taxes: your Social Security number, your W-2 form from your employer (this form shows how much you've earned and how much you've already paid in taxes), and any other documents that report income, like interest statements from banks or dividends from investments.

Common Deductions and Credits for Young Adults

Deductions and credits are like discount coupons and VIP passes for your taxes; they can reduce how much you owe. As a young adult, you might qualify for a few valuable ones:

1. Education Credits: If you're in college, you might be eligible for the American Opportunity Credit or the Lifetime Learning Credit, which can help lower your bill if you've been paying for tuition or textbooks.
2. Standard Deduction: For 2021, this is $12,550 for single filers. It reduces the income you're taxed on.

Using Tax Software vs. Hiring a Professional

Deciding whether to use tax software or hire a tax professional is like choosing between DIYing a meal with a meal kit or going to a restaurant. Tax software is less expensive and could be a great choice if your tax situation isn't too complicated. Think of it as a recipe. Hiring a professional, like dining out, is more costly but might be worth it if your tax situation is complex or you want the assurance of having an expert handle it.

Eligible Deductions for Teens

Even as a teenager, you might have deductions available. If you've had a summer job or worked after school, you can deduct unreimbursed work-related expenses. Plus, if you've been stashing some of your earnings into a Roth IRA, kudos to you—that's a savvy move for your future.

Strategies for Maximizing Returns

To maximize your tax return, think of squeezing every bit of juice from an orange. Make sure you're taking advantage of all deductions and credits you qualify for. Keep good records throughout the year. It's like keeping score in a game; it helps you know where you stand when it's time to file.

If you're running a business, I strongly recommend using a CPA who can help you do all the tax deductions. If you don't own a business, there aren't many tax deductions you qualify for. Every situation is different, so do your due diligence.

Avoiding Audits

An audit is when the IRS decides to check that all the information on your tax return is correct. Think of it as a teacher asking you to show your work on a tricky math problem. To avoid audits, make sure you report all your income, only claim deductions and credits you qualify for, and file on time.

Interactive Element: Tax Checklist

To keep you organized and ensure you have everything you need to file, here's a handy checklist:

1. Gather all income documents (W-2s, 1099s, etc.)
2. Collect receipts for eligible deductions (educational expenses, work-related costs)
3. Decide if you're using tax software or hiring a professional
4. Check the IRS website for any new credits or deductions.
5. File your taxes by April 15th

Use this checklist as your pre-game warm-up to ensure you're prepared to tackle your taxes.

Filing taxes isn't the most exhilarating part of adulting, but understanding how to navigate them leaves more money in your wallet and fewer worries on your mind. So, take a deep breath, gather your documents, and remember it's just another puzzle to solve, and you've got this!

10.2 TAX-ADVANTAGED ACCOUNTS AND INVESTMENTS FOR YOUNG ADULTS

Imagine your money grows without the constant nagging of taxes each step of the way. That's the deal with tax-advantaged accounts like Roth IRAs and 401(k)s. These accounts are like financial greenhouses; they provide a sheltered environment where your investments grow more robustly, shielded from the tax winds outside.

Why should you, a young adult, get excited about Roth IRAs and 401(k)s? First off, these accounts provide tantalizing tax benefits that help your savings multiply faster. With a Roth IRA, for example, you pay taxes on the money you contribute upfront. It might sound like a downer initially, but here's the kicker: your money grows tax-free, and you don't pay a dime in taxes when you withdraw it during retirement. It's like planting seeds you've already paid for and harvesting the crops at no extra cost. On the other hand, a traditional 401(k) lets you postpone paying taxes on the money you contribute until you retire, which means you can invest more of your income now and potentially reduce your current tax bill.

Both Roth IRAs and 401(k)s have specific eligibility criteria and contribution limits. For Roth IRAs, your ability to contribute depends on your income level. Generally, the more you earn, the less you might be able to contribute, and if you earn too much, you might not be able to contribute directly at all. For 2023, if you're single, you can contribute the full amount if your income is under $138,000. For 401(k)s, the rules are more about how much you can stash away annually. In 2023, you can contribute up to $22,500, and if you're under 50, you can throw in an extra $7,500 as a catch-up contribution.

Choosing where to park your money within these accounts is like picking the right dance floor based on the music you like. It's all about matching your investment choices to your personal financial goals and how much risk you're comfortable taking on. If you're the type who likes a steady beat, you might lean toward more conservative investments like bonds. If you can handle a bit of a mosh pit, stocks or stock mutual funds might be more your style. Most platforms offering these accounts provide a range of investment options, and some even have targeted retirement funds that adjust the mix of stocks and bonds as you get closer to retirement, making the investment decision more accessible and adaptive to your needs.

Withdrawal Rules

While these accounts provide fantastic perks, there's a catch—withdrawal rules. For Roth IRAs, you can withdraw your contributions anytime tax-free and penalty-free, which is fantastic. However, pulling out your earnings before age 59½ might result in taxes and penalties unless you meet specific exceptions, like buying your first home. For 401(k)s, early withdrawals can also lead to taxes and penalties, though there are some exceptions here too, like severe financial hardship. The key is to understand these rules thoroughly to avoid any financial hangovers.

Navigating the world of tax-advantaged accounts doesn't have to be daunting. By understanding the benefits, rules, and strategies for investing within these accounts, you're setting yourself up for a wealthier retirement and a financially sound present.

Remember the essence of what we've covered: these financial vehicles have powerful ways to grow your wealth while optimizing your tax situation. Whether it's a Roth IRA, a traditional 401(k), or other tax-advantaged options, the key is to start early, contribute regularly, and choose your investments based on your risk tolerance and financial goals. By doing so, you're building a foundation for a secure future.

CHAPTER 11

OVERCOMING FINANCIAL ANXIETY

Y ou're about to hit the checkout button on an online store, and your cart is full of items you've been eyeing for weeks. Suddenly, your stomach knots up, your palms get sweaty, and a barrage of worries floods your mind. Can I afford this? What if I need this money for something else? Yep, that's financial anxiety knocking at your door, and trust me, it's not delivering a package you want to keep.

11.1 IDENTIFYING AND OVERCOMING FINANCIAL ANXIETY

Understanding Financial Anxiety

Financial anxiety is a formidable opponent. It's not about feeling overwhelmed by bills or student loans; it's about how this stress influences your daily choices and peace of mind. It can make you question every purchase or keep you awake at night pondering if you'll ever achieve financial security. This type of anxiety impacts your mental health and your ability to make rational money decisions. But here's the empowering part: by understanding it, you take control.

Common Triggers

What lights the fuse for this anxiety? For many young adults, debt is a biggie. Whether it's student loans, credit card debt, money you owe to friends, etc., debt can feel like a shadow looming over your future. Another trigger? Uncertain income. If your job situation feels as stable as a Jenga tower in a windstorm, that uncertainty can be an enormous source of stress. It's tough to plan when you're unsure what you'll earn next month.

Mindfulness and Financial Anxiety

Here's good news: you can manage this anxiety. One powerful tool is mindfulness. Yes, mindfulness, the art of staying present and engaged in the current moment, can also be applied to how you handle your finances. It's about observing your financial habits and emotions without judgment. Next time you feel that anxiety creeping up when you're about to make a financial decision, take a deep breath. Ask yourself: Is this anxiety based on immediate financial danger, or is it old fears and uncertainties playing tricks on me? This pause can help you respond to the situation with clarity rather than fear.

Seeking Professional Help

There may be times when the weight of financial anxiety feels too much to bear alone, and that's fine. In fact, it's a sign of strength to recognize when you need support. That is where a professional can be your best investment.

Financial therapists are experts in helping people understand and improve the psychological aspects of their financial decisions. If your financial anxiety is overwhelming, reaching out to a therapist who provides financial counseling could be a game-changer. They can equip you with tools to manage your anxiety and guide you toward a healthier relationship with money.

Interactive Element: Financial Anxiety Journal Prompt

To help you start on the path to managing financial anxiety, here's a journal prompt: Write down three financial fears you have. Next to each, note whether it's a current reality or a potential scenario.

This exercise can help you pinpoint where your anxieties are coming from and how much they align with your actual financial situation.

11.2 BUILDING FINANCIAL RESISTANCE: TIPS AND SUCCESS STORIES

Financial resilience is like your financial immune system. A strong immune system keeps you healthy, and financial resilience helps you handle and bounce back from monetary setbacks. Life throws curveballs like unexpected car repairs, medical emergencies, or job losses. Financial resilience means you're prepared to catch these curveballs without them knocking you off your game, and you can do that with the tips mentioned earlier: start a part-time job, freelance gigs, a side business, investments, etc. Together, these streams form a robust financial river.

Applying Resilience to Real Life

Let's talk real-life examples—nothing like seeing resilience in action to get inspired. Take Clara, a graphic designer who found herself out of work when her company downsized. Instead of panicking, she tapped into her resilience. She had always done freelance work on the side, and it became her primary income source. But Clara didn't stop there. She diversified further by teaching online courses. That brought in extra income and solidified her reputation in the design community. Within a year, she earned more than she did at her previous job, proving that with resilience, a setback can set the stage for a comeback.

Community Help

Community support is a cornerstone in constructing and maintaining financial resilience. It's about the connections you make and the support you receive. Networking isn't merely about finding jobs; it's about fostering relationships that bring guidance, advice, and opportunities.

Joining local or online groups related to your career field can open doors you didn't know existed. Attending workshops and seminars helps you learn and connects you with like-minded individuals instrumental in your journey to financial resilience. The stronger your community, the stronger your financial health.

Finding Resources

There's a wealth of information out there, from books and podcasts about personal finance to online courses on money management and investing. Libraries and community centers provide free workshops. Websites like the Financial Independence Forum provide platforms for advice and support from peers who are also working toward financial resilience. Leveraging these resources can provide you with the knowledge and tools to build your financial strength.

11.3 FROM PANIC TO POWER: TRANSFORMING FINANCIAL MISTAKES INTO LEARNING OPPORTUNITIES

Picture this: You're playing your favorite video game, and you've missed a jump—game over. But here's the thing: you get another shot, and maybe you learn a trick or two about how to leap better next time. That's like handling financial mistakes. They're not the end of the world; they're part of learning how to play the game of life smarter. So, let's shift our perspective on financial blunders. Instead of seeing them as disasters, view them as valuable lessons gearing you up for success.

Financial Oops Moments

Let's dissect these financial oops moments. It starts with detective work. You'll want to roll back the tape and look at what led to the mistake. Was it a spontaneous spending spree that drained your savings? Perhaps it was an investment in what promised to be a high-return venture but ended up being a financial sinkhole? Analyzing these moments can reveal patterns or trigger points. For instance, maybe you tend to overspend in social settings, under the influence of friends who love splurging. Perhaps you've realized that more research is needed before investing is a recurring theme. Understanding these patterns is your first step in preventing future financial facepalms.

Financial Comebacks

Crafting your comeback is next. That is your plan to not only bounce back but spring forward. Start by setting clear, achievable financial goals. If you've run up debt, your initial aim might be setting up a new budget that allocates more to debt repayment. If a risky investment sets you back, you may decide to educate yourself on investment strategies or seek advice from a financial advisor. This part of your journey is about rebuilding stronger. Think of it as upgrading your armor in that video game. You want to ensure that next time you're better protected and more resilient.

The Growth Mindset

Maintaining a growth mindset is crucial and is about believing your abilities and intelligence can develop over time. It's the opposite of thinking, "I'm bad with money," and shutting the door on potential growth. With a growth mindset, every financial setback is a springboard for development. It's about asking, "What can I learn from this?" rather than, "Why does this always happen to me?" This outlook will help you manage money more effectively and improve your resilience and adaptability.

By embracing your errors, analyzing their roots, crafting a solid comeback plan, and fostering a growth mindset, you transform from a financial rookie to a savvy player. Remember, every financial failure has the potential to be your stepping stone to success, so next time you slip up, recognize it, learn from it, and get ready to level up.

11.4 THE ROLE OF MONEY IN HAPPINESS: A BALANCED VIEW

Let's get honest about money and happiness. It's like that old saying, "Money can't buy happiness," but money can certainly buy you a ticket to a championship game of your favorite sport. So, what's the real deal here? How does the cash in your wallet translate into smiles on your face? Money undeniably influences our well-being, but it's not a magic potion that erases all worries. Instead, think of it as a tool—a useful one—that, when used wisely, can help construct a more comfortable, joyful life.

Money and Well-being

The connection between money and happiness isn't about the numbers in your bank account but how those numbers affect your day-to-day life. When you have enough money to cover your basic needs—food, shelter, healthcare—the stress in your life can decrease. It's like having a good pair of hiking boots. They don't make the mountain any smaller, but they sure make climbing it a lot more comfortable.

Once these basic needs are met, extra dollars have a smaller impact on your overall happiness. This phenomenon is known as the 'law of diminishing returns'. Basically, the more you have, the less each additional dollar improves your happiness.

Think about it this way: buying a new smartphone can give you a happiness boost, but the thrill fades quickly. Yet, being able to afford a doctor's visit or fixing a broken car without financial strain provides a more profound and enduring sense of security and satisfaction. Here, money isn't directly buying happiness; it's buying peace of mind, which is a vital ingredient for happiness.

The Limitations of Wealth

Beyond a certain point, wealth accumulates, and happiness levels plateau. That doesn't mean wealthy people aren't or can't be happy, but it highlights that additional wealth is less likely to impact their happiness. It's like when you eat your favorite pizza; the first few slices are delightful, but as you keep eating, additional slices seem less satisfying.

This concept is imperative to grasp because it helps you set realistic expectations about what money can and cannot do for you. If you're chasing a massive bank balance thinking it will solve all your problems, you might end up disappointed. Instead, if you focus on how you use your resources to create a fulfilling life, you're likely to find more joy. That means investing in experiences, relationships, and goals that align with who you are and want to be.

Purposeful Spending

Finally, let's consider purposeful spending. This is about making financial choices that reflect your values and contribute to your long-term well-being. It's choosing to spend money on a gym membership because you value health or buying a durable, well-made backpack rather than a cheaper, throw-away alternative because sustainability is important to you. Every choice reflects personal values and contributes to happiness.

Purposeful spending also means sometimes choosing generosity. Studies suggest that spending money on others can boost your happiness. Whether it's buying coffee for a friend or donating to a charity that resonates with your values, these acts of kindness make the world better while making you feel good.

The Relationship Between Money and Happiness

Money's role in happiness is important, but not everything. It's less about the amount and more about how you manage and spend it. By understanding these dynamics, you can use your financial resources to enhance your well-being and bring genuine joy. As we move forward, let's explore how to leverage financial tools for wealth creation and crafting a more fulfilling life.

CHAPTER 12
UTILIZING FINANCIAL TECHNOLOGY

I magine this: you're amid a bustling metropolis, like Tokyo, with its myriad of sights, sounds, and flavors. Venturing through this vibrant city without a map or your trusty smartphone GPS would be difficult, right? That's like managing your finances without the empowering assistance of financial technology. Today, FinTech isn't just a convenient tool—it's your financial GPS, empowering you to navigate the complexities of budgeting, investing, and saving with confidence and control.

12.1 BUDGETING AND INVESTING APPS: WHAT'S OUT THERE?

Overview of Financial Apps

In the sprawling app stores brimming with applications, financial apps are like the neon lights in Times Square—they stand out because they promise to make your monetary management more effective. However, it's important to note that while these apps can be useful, they come with their set of risks, but for now, let's focus on the pros.

From budgeting basics to complex investment portfolios, there's an app designed to cater to your every financial need. Whether you're saving up for that dream car, trying to keep your coffee budget under control, or investing in stocks for the first time, these apps are like having a financial advisor right in your pocket.

First and foremost, as mentioned before, budgeting apps like Mint and YNAB (You Need A Budget) are the superheroes of money management. I strongly recommend using apps like this early. They assist you in tracking every dollar earned and spent, categorizing your expenses, and setting up savings goals.

Investing apps like Robinhood and Acorns enable you to buy and sell stocks without hefty fees and educate you on the fundamentals of stock markets with their user-friendly interfaces. For those with specific savings goals, such as a rainy-day fund or a round-the-world trip, apps like Digit and Qapital automate your savings.

App Reviews and Comparisons

Let's break down a few favorites, starting with Mint. Known for its comprehensive budgeting tools and real-time tracking, Mint is fantastic for getting a bird's eye view of your finances. However, if you're looking for something with more in-depth budgeting and hands-on planning, YNAB is your ticket. It's designed to give you a forward-looking approach to budgeting, teaching you to "give every dollar a job."

For investing newbies, Robinhood has become synonymous with beginner investing thanks to its user-friendly interface and zero-commission trades. But if you're interested in getting some micro-investing done, Acorns is more up your alley. It rounds your purchases to the nearest dollar and invests the spare change in a diversified portfolio.

Integrating Apps into Daily Life

So, you've picked an app or two—now what? Integrating these apps into your routine is critical to getting the most out of them. Start by setting aside a few minutes each day to check your transactions and budgets. That can be as simple as reviewing your expenses over coffee in the morning. Make it a habit to categorize your expenses as they happen.

Next, utilize notifications and alerts. Most apps have features that alert you when you're nearing a budget limit or if there's unusual activity in your account. These can be lifesavers, especially if you're prone to overspending or keeping a tight leash on your finances.

Lastly, don't forget to sync your financial apps with your financial goals. If your goal is saving for a new car, set that specific goal in your savings app and track your progress. Seeing the numbers climb is motivating and can turn the tedious task of saving money into a thrilling race to the finish line.

Interactive Element: Financial App Exploration Exercise

To get you started, here's a simple exercise: Download one budgeting app and one investing app. Spend a week familiarizing yourself with their features. Track all your expenses and play around with making a small investment. At the end of the week, reflect on how these apps impacted your view of managing money. What did you find helpful? What felt challenging? This hands-on approach will boost your confidence in using financial technology and empower you to take control of your financial future.

In the ever-evolving landscape of personal finance, financial technology is your ally, making difficult tasks manageable and complex concepts understandable. By embracing these tools, you're stepping ahead with knowledge and skills that turn financial management into an adventure. Let these apps be your guide, coach, and cheerleader. Keep exploring, keep learning, and most importantly, keep pushing your financial boundaries.

12.2 THE FUTURE OF MONEY: NFTS EXPLAINED

Let's crack the code on a massive buzz word in finance: NFTs, or Non-Fungible Tokens. Think of them as one-of-a-kind collector's items but in digital form. Whether it's a piece of digital art, a music file, or even a tweet, NFTs transform digital works into unique, verifiable assets that can be bought and sold like any other piece of property but have no tangible form of their own.

The "non-fungible" means they're unique and can't be replaced with something else. For example, a bitcoin is fungible—trade one for another bitcoin and you'll have the same thing. A one-of-a-kind trading card, however, is non-fungible. If you traded it for a different card, you'd have something different. This uniqueness is what has catapulted NFTs to stardom in the art world and beyond.

Speculating on how NFTs will impact personal finance and transactions in the long run can feel like predicting the next season's hottest fashion trend. However, it's clear they are carving a transformative path. They challenge the traditional financial frameworks and open a new realm of digital economic interactions.

NFTs redefine concepts of ownership and copyright, offering artists and creators a new way to monetize their work directly.

NFTs aren't fleeting trends; they're the frontiers of the digital financial revolution. As we continue to navigate this exciting yet unpredictable terrain, the key will be to approach with curiosity, caution, and a willingness to learn.

Next up is the gig economy. Get ready to explore flexible work options that offer freedom and personal growth and present new challenges in managing income and benefits.

CHAPTER 13
THE GIG ECONOMY
AND YOU

Think of the gig economy as the ultimate choose-your-own-adventure book, but instead of flipping pages, you're clicking through job listings. It's where traditional 9-to-5s take a backseat, and flexible, short-term jobs grab the wheel.

Whether you're delivering meals, designing websites from your bedroom, or driving folks around your city, gig work could be your ticket to a more dynamic way of working.

13.1 MAXIMIZING YOUR EARNINGS IN THE GIG ECONOMY

Finding Lucrative Gigs: Tips for Finding and Securing High-Paying Gigs in Various Industries

The secret sauce to thriving in the gig economy is knowing where to look for the best opportunities. Start with niche platforms that align with your skills. For instance, if you're a graphic designer, websites like Behance or Dribbble can connect you with high-quality gigs that match your expertise. Similarly, techies can check out platforms like TopTal or GitHub Jobs for gigs that require serious coding skills.

Networking is another option where you can dive into online communities relevant to your field on platforms like Reddit or join Facebook groups where gig opportunities are shared.

Don't underestimate the power of a good old-fashioned word-of-mouth recommendation, either. Let friends, family, and professional connections know what you're up to. Sometimes, the best gigs come from someone who knows someone who heard you're awesome at what you do.

Negotiating Rates: Strategies for Negotiating Pay Rates and Terms to Ensure Fair Compensation

Negotiating feels like stepping into a wild jungle if you're not used to it, but it's one of the imperative skills that boosts your gig earnings.

First, know your worth. Research the going rates for the services you promote. Websites like Glassdoor and Payscale can provide insights into market standards. Armed with this knowledge, you can state your rates without underselling yourself.

When discussing rates with potential clients, be clear about what those rates include and any conditions that might affect pricing, such as rush fees or revisions. Always put agreements in writing— yes, a formal contract. That might seem like overkill, but it protects both parties and ensures there are no surprises about payment down the line.

Using Technology to Find Work: Overview of Platforms and Apps that Connect Gig Workers with Opportunities

In today's tech-savvy world, finding gig work is at the tip of your fingers. Apps and platforms are the matchmakers of the gig economy, connecting you with those in need of your mad skills. For general gig work, apps like TaskRabbit and Fiverr have a plethora of options, from furniture assembly to freelance writing. Ride-sharing giants like Uber and Lyft are perfect for those who prefer to make money behind the wheel.

For something more specific, like pet sitting, Rover might be your go-to. These platforms help you find work and handle the pesky parts like payments and billing, so you can focus more on the work and less on the logistics. Just remember, while these apps open doors to numerous opportunities, they also take a cut of your earnings, so always read the fine print and plan your finances accordingly.

Interactive Element: Gig Opportunity Brainstorming Exercise

To get your gears turning, here's a quick exercise. Grab a sheet of paper, or open a new digital note, and jot down all your skills and passions. Next to each, brainstorm at least two types of gig work that could align with those skills. For example, if you love writing and technology, consider tech blogging or creating content for tech companies' blogs. This exercise can help you visualize potential gig paths and spark ideas for diversifying your gig portfolio.

13.2 FINANCIAL MANAGEMENT FOR GIG WORKERS: TAXES, SAVINGS, AND INSURANCE

Discovering the financial waters of gig work can sometimes feel like trying to play a guitar solo without ever learning to play the guitar. You've got irregular income that ebbs and flows, tax situations that could make your head spin, and the looming question of how to handle things like insurance and retirement without a traditional safety net. Let's break down these concepts into manageable chords so you can rock your finances.

Managing Irregular Income: Techniques for Budgeting and Saving When Income Fluctuates

Dealing with an income that swings more than a pendulum in a grandfather clock requires clever budgeting tactics. Think of your income as a series of peaks and valleys. During peaks, you feel like a rock star, but those valleys make you feel more like a one-hit-wonder. To even out the ride, start with a baseline budget based on your average income over the last six to twelve months. This average gives you a realistic view of what you typically earn rather than planning around those top-earning months.

Once you have your baseline, create a buffer by squirreling away extra cash during the flush times. This buffer acts like an economic shock absorber, helping you manage during leaner months without altering your lifestyle or falling into debt. Tools like automatic savings apps can be your best friend here, pulling money into savings without you having to lift a finger when you're earning more.

Tax Obligations and Deductions: Explain Tax Responsibilities for Gig Workers and Potential Deductions to Lower Tax Bills

If you're gigging, you're running your own business, meaning you're responsible for your taxes, including making quarterly estimated tax payments to the IRS. Getting cozy with a tax professional can be a lifesaver. They help you with the complexities of self-employment taxes and keep enough of your earnings aside to not get hit with penalties when tax time rolls around.

But it's not all take and no give; there are sweet tax deductions available that can help reduce how much you owe. You can deduct business expenses like the cost of your laptop, travel expenses to gigs, or even part of your rent if you have a home office. Keeping meticulous records of these expenses is key. Apps that track spending and categorize expenses are handy, turning what could be a nightmare of paperwork into a streamlined part of your routine.

Insurance Needs: Discuss the Types of Insurance Gig Workers Should Consider to Protect Themselves Financially

Insurance might not be the first thing on your mind when hustling from gig to gig, but it's a critical part of your financial toolkit. Without the safety net of employer-provided benefits, you're responsible for insurance. Start with health insurance; an unexpected medical bill without coverage can be financially devastating. Thanks to marketplaces under the Affordable Care Act, you can find a range of plans that might fit your budget and needs.

Don't stop there, though. Consider disability insurance, which can protect your income if you're unable to work due to injury or illness. And if you're really thinking ahead, investigate liability insurance, especially if your gig work involves a risk to others (think driving passengers around or performing at venues). These policies can help cover costs if you're ever sued for damages or injuries related to your work.

Retirement Planning: Options for Gig Workers to Plan for Retirement Without a Traditional Employer-Sponsored Plan

Finally, let's talk about your encore—retirement. Without a traditional employer-sponsored retirement plan, it's up to you to set the stage for your golden years. Individual Retirement Accounts (IRAs) are a great start. You can choose between a traditional IRA, which offers tax-deferred growth, or a Roth IRA, where you pay taxes on contributions upfront but withdraw money tax-free in retirement. If you're catching your stride in the gig economy, a solo 401(k) might be a better fit, allowing you to save much more per year than traditional IRAs.

Consider setting up automatic contributions to your retirement accounts, timed with your income spikes. That way, you're building your retirement fund without thinking. Investing in a diversified portfolio can help grow your savings over time, turning gig income into a substantial nest egg.

With the proper techniques for managing irregular income, understanding your tax obligations, securing necessary insurance, and planning for retirement, you can hit all the right notes and enjoy the gig life. Whether you're a starting or a seasoned gig worker, taking control of these elements can lead to a more stable and financially sound career.

13.3 FINDING STABILITY THROUGH GIG WORK

The gig economy feels like a wide-open road with its share of potholes. One major challenge is the financial instability that comes with the territory. Unlike traditional jobs, gig work doesn't guarantee a steady paycheck. Your earnings fluctuate based on the season, the economy, or health. And then there's the lack of benefits. Health insurance, paid leave, retirement plans—all the safety nets that come with full-time employment are usually on you to manage, which can be intimidating if you're not a planning pro.

So, how do you build stability in this unstable landscape? Start by treating your gig work like a business. That means meticulous financial planning and management. Create a budget that accounts for your variable income and includes a line item for savings, acting as your safety net for slower months. It's also smart to diversify your income streams. Don't rely on one type of gig or platform. Spread your talents across several to avoid the financial dip that can come if one dries up.

Looking at the bigger picture, what does a career look like in the gig economy? It's not your traditional climb-the-corporate-ladder scenario. Career advancement in gig work requires a proactive approach. You might start with smaller gigs, and as you build your reputation, you can leverage your portfolio to secure more lucrative projects. The more you can offer, the more marketable you are. That might mean taking online courses to boost your skills or attending workshops and conferences to stay on top of industry trends.

Like any choice, gig work comes with its trade-offs. Balancing freedom and flexibility with the need for financial stability and growth is your focus here to guarantee you enjoy the rhythm without getting lost in the shuffle.

While the path may seem fraught with uncertainties, it brims with opportunities. The skills you develop, the flexibility you enjoy, and the resilience you build here are invaluable.

CHAPTER 14

FINANCIAL LITERACY FOR ENTREPRENEURS

P icture a carnival where you're at a booth where you can win a prize if you knock all the cans down. Starting a business is like that—it's thrilling, a bit unpredictable, and ultimately, you could walk away with something incredible. But instead of tossing a ball at a stack of cans, you're hurling your skills, passion, and clever planning into the mix, hoping it'll knock down the barriers to success. Let's dive into the financial nuts and bolts that will help you keep your eye on the prize and confirm you're ready to win.

14.1 STARTING YOUR BUSINESS: THE FINANCIAL BASICS

Business Planning and Financial Forecasting

First things first: your business plan is your roadmap. It's not just a document for attracting investors; it's your blueprint for understanding your market, defining your goals, and plotting your growth. Think of it as your business's weather forecast, helping you prepare for the sunny days of profit and the stormy times when cash flow might tighten.

Creating a financial forecast isn't about pulling numbers out of thin air. It's about grounding your entrepreneurial dreams. Start with your revenue projections—how much money you expect to make from your products or services. Then, chart your expected expenses, like rent, supplies, and salaries. The difference will give you a preliminary glimpse at potential profits or the need for a tighter belt.

Managing Startup Costs

Keep a keen eye on your startup costs. These initial expenses can be like a wild garden hose—hard to control and capable of spraying money in every direction. To clamp down, categorize your costs into 'essential' and 'nice-to-have.' Essentials are your must-pays, like licensing fees or essential equipment. Nice-to-haves? They can wait. Remember, every dollar you save invests into growing your business.

Leverage technology to find cost-effective solutions. Need business cards? Maybe start with a digital version before going for high-grade printed ones. Marketing can also start small with social media campaigns before scaling up as your business grows. This cautious approach helps you avoid splurging on unnecessary expenses that can bog down your financial runway before you even take off.

Separating Personal and Business Finances

Here's a golden rule: Keep your personal and business finances as separate as pineapple and pizza—some people might mix them, but it's not for everyone, and it can get messy. Opening a business bank account is step one. Not only does this help you track your business transactions cleanly, but it also presents a professional front to your customers and suppliers.

Separating finances helps during tax season. It simplifies deductions and can protect your assets from business liabilities. Think of it as building a firewall between your personal life and business operations; it's essential for safeguarding both.

Essential Financial Management Tools

In today's digital age, skipping out on financial management tools is like trying to row a boat with your hands—inefficient. Tools like QuickBooks or FreshBooks offer robust platforms for managing invoices, expenditures, and payroll. They can automate what used to be a headache of paperwork, allowing you more time to focus on growing your business.

Consider tools for project management like Trello or Asana. While not financial tools per se, they help keep your projects and budget on track. They're like having an assistant who reminds you of what's due, what's over budget, and what needs immediate attention.

Interactive Element: Financial Tool Exploration Exercise

To get hands-on with your financial management learning curve, here's a simple exercise. Choose one financial and project management tool from the suggestions above. Most offer free trials, so sign up and spend a week or two getting to know them. Use the financial tool to create a sample budget for a hypothetical project and the project management tool to outline the steps to complete it. This exercise will familiarize you with the tools and give you a taste of the clarity and control they can bring to your business operations.

Starting your enterprise is an adventure, and like any good adventure, preparation is critical. By understanding the financial fundamentals, you'll set up your business for success and enjoy the ride more.

14.2 FINANCING YOUR STARTUP: FROM BOOTSTRAPPING TO VENTURE CAPITAL

So, you've got a killer business idea that's as exciting as deciding what toppings to put on your pizza on a Saturday night, but how do you fund this dream? Let's walk through the candy store of financing options, from the humble piggy bank method to the big-league investors, and see what sweetness each can bring to your startup, along with a few inevitable cavities.

Overview of Financing Options

Starting with bootstrapping—this is your DIY project. It means pulling yourself up by your bootstraps, using your savings, or maybe some cash from a day job to fund your venture. It's great because you retain total control over your business, and your company remains debt-free, but it can be slow.

Then, there's the option of taking out loans. Imagine this as asking your friend to lend you money for a project, but this friend is a bank and wants their money back—with interest. Loans are convenient when you need a substantial cash injection that bootstrapping can't cover. They can kickstart your business growth much quicker than saving up little by little. However, they also come with strings attached, like repayment schedules and interest rates, which can feel like a backpack full of bricks if cash flow slows down.

Meanwhile, venture capital is like auditioning in front of judges on a talent show. Investors give you funding in exchange for equity in your company. If your business is the next big thing, these investors are your golden ticket. They not only provide money but can also offer valuable advice and connections. The downside? You're giving away a slice of your pie, and with investors involved, decisions are no longer yours alone.

Pros and Cons of Each Financing Method

Bootstrapping is fantastic for staying debt-free and keeping control, but it's a slow burn. It tests your endurance and might limit how quickly you can scale your operations. Loans provide a quicker pathway to significant funds, allowing for rapid growth and potentially big moves like major equipment purchases or prime real estate acquisitions. But debt is a tricky dance partner, especially if your business hits a rough patch.

Venture capital can propel your business into the stratosphere, contributing funds, mentorship, and industry doors that would otherwise be tough to open. However, it means sharing your vision and possibly diverging from your original path based on your investors' strategies and expectations.

Pitching to Investors

When you pitch to investors, think of it as preparing for the most important performance of your life. You're the main act, and the stage is yours. First, know your audience. Research your potential investors—understand their interests, past investments, and industry expertise. Tailor your pitch to resonate with them, like choosing a playlist your road trip buddies will love.

Your pitch itself should be a compelling story. Start with the problem your business solves, introduce your unique solution, and highlight your market potential. Be clear, be concise, and above all, be passionate. Then, show your traction. That includes anything from sales figures to user growth metrics or strategic partnerships. And don't paint the skies pink; be upfront about the risks, too. Investors will appreciate your transparency and realism.

Crowdfunding

Lastly, let's not forget crowdfunding—the digital age's answer to funding. Platforms like Kickstarter or Indiegogo allow you to pitch your business to the world. It's like throwing a massive party and asking each guest to bring a dish. Only here, the dishes are small investments from a giant audience. Crowdfunding raises funds, validates your business concept, and builds a community of supporters invested in your success.

The beauty of crowdfunding is its ability to generate buzz and engage with potential customers before you launch. However, it requires a killer marketing strategy and a tangible product or prototype that excites people. And remember, it's not just about reaching the funding goal; it's about fulfilling those promises.

Delivering on your commitments is crucial to maintaining trust and credibility in the market.

Whether you're bootstrapping with your savings, pitching to sharks in suits, taking on loans, or rallying the internet crowd, each method proposes unique benefits and challenges. Choose wisely, plan meticulously, and always keep your end goal in sight —launching and growing a business that makes a mark.

14.3 MANAGING BUSINESS FINANCES: KEEPING PERSONAL AND BUSINESS SEPARATE

Maintaining financial discipline is critical for the health and success of your business. Think of financial discipline as the backbone of your entrepreneurial body since it keeps everything upright and functioning. Without it, your business is vulnerable like a jellyfish.

Establish A Business Banking Account

First, you'll want to establish a business banking account to keep your personal and business finances distinct. Imagine this scenario: you're at a fancy restaurant, and when it's time to pay, you accidentally whip out your business card instead of your personal one. Oops! That's a minor blip, but mix-ups can get messier, especially with taxes in the mix. A separate business account avoids these blunders and simplifies financial tracking and reporting.

Setting up a business bank account is usually straightforward. You'll need paperwork like business registration and EIN (employer identification number). While you're at it, getting a business credit card can be a smart move, too. Not only does it help build your business credit score, but it can also come with perks like cashback or travel rewards, which could be a nice little bonus for your business expenses. Here is a QR code on how to open a business bank account. Note, almost no bank will let you open a bank account without creating your entity first (LLC, S-Cop, C-Corp, etc.)

Bookkeeping

Now, onto the glamorous world of bookkeeping. Okay, it's not that glamorous, but it's essential. Keeping accurate records of every transaction in your business is the golden rule here. That means documenting your income, expenses, debts, and investments. Efficient bookkeeping practices are like having a detailed map of your business journey; they show you where you're doing great and where you might be leaking money without realizing it.

You don't need to be a math wizard for bookkeeping. Thanks to modern software like Xero, QuickBooks, or simpler tools like Excel spreadsheets, bookkeeping is manageable. These tools automate the grunt work, from categorizing expenses to generating financial reports. That keeps you sane during tax season and gives you valuable insights into your business finances, allowing you to make informed decisions rather than guessing your way through.

Entrepreneur Tax Obligations

Speaking of taxes, let's talk about your tax obligations as an entrepreneur. Unlike being an employee, where taxes are typically taken from your paycheck, managing your taxes as a business owner is on you. You'll need to know quarterly tax payments, deductions, and liability. It might sound daunting, but understanding these elements confirms you're not caught off guard by a hefty tax bill or legal penalties.

Efficient tax planning involves more than just meeting deadlines. It's about strategically managing your taxable income. That could mean taking advantage of business deductions like home office expenses, travel, or even educational workshops that improve your business acumen. Every dollar you save on taxes reinvests into growing your business. Consider consulting with a tax professional who can assure you're using all the available strategies to minimize your tax liability while staying compliant with the IRS.

Entrepreneurship is about being proactive rather than reactive, keeping your business's financial health in check, and setting the stage for sustainable growth and success. As we close this chapter on financial literacy for entrepreneurs, take these insights and tools and apply them diligently.

CHAPTER 15
UNDERSTANDING GLOBAL ECONOMICS

I magine you're a surfer out on the ocean, waiting for that perfect wave. You watch as waves form, grow, and eventually break before you choose the right one to ride. Similarly, the global economy is like the ocean, with waves of economic cycles. As a financial surfer, understanding these waves is essential to keep from wiping out and catching the best waves that propel you toward your financial goals.

15.1 THE IMPACT OF ECONOMIC CYCLES ON YOUR FINANCES

Understanding Economic Cycles

Economic cycles, also called business cycles, are the fluctuations the economy goes through. These cycles are marked by four main phases: expansion, peak, contraction, and trough. During an expansion, the economy grows, as evidenced by increased jobs, consumer spending, and production. The peak is the height of this growth before the economy slows. Contraction, or recession, is when the economy shrinks, leading to decreased spending and higher unemployment. Finally, the trough is the lowest point of the cycle, after which things pick up again.

These phases impact the job market, interest rates, and inflation. For example, during an expansion, you might see more job openings and rising wages as businesses grow. Conversely, during a contraction, jobs might be harder to come by, and wages could stagnate or decrease. Interest rates typically fall during a recession as the government tries to encourage more spending by making borrowing cheaper. Meanwhile, inflation rates can fluctuate, frequently rising during a booming economy due to increased consumer spending and falling during a recession as demand drops.

Recession-proofing Your Finances

How do you safeguard your finances when economic tides turn rough? As mentioned earlier, it's wise to establish an emergency fund. Think of this as your financial life jacket, keeping you afloat during times when income might drop or become less reliable. Ideally, this fund should cover 3-6 months of living expenses. Next, diversify your income streams to protect your income from getting completely wiped out during financial emergencies.

Another strategy is focusing on reducing high-interest debt during economic strong points. That lessens your financial obligations and frees up more of your income to save or invest. Also, keep your resume updated and your skills sharp. Continuous learning and adaptability can make you more marketable, helping you scour a tough job market more effectively.

Capitalizing on Economic Recoveries

Like surfers using the momentum of a wave to ride to shore, you can use economic recoveries to accelerate your financial growth. When the economy begins to recover, it's a good time to search for new job opportunities or ask for a raise, as businesses may be expanding and investing in new talent. It's also an opportune moment to invest in stocks or real estate, as prices might still be lower from the recession phase.

Furthermore, consider increasing your contributions to retirement accounts during these times. With the economy on the upswing, your investments have a higher chance to grow.

Long-term Planning and Economic Trends

Understanding and planning for economic cycles is like setting out to sea with a map and compass. It requires preparation and a long-term perspective. Recognize that economic downturns are normal, albeit challenging, parts of the economic cycle. By planning for these downturns, you can avoid making short-sighted decisions based on fear or panic.

Keep an eye on broader economic trends and indicators such as GDP growth rates, unemployment rates, and consumer spending patterns. That gives you clues about where the economy might be headed and help you adjust your financial strategies accordingly. The goal is not just to survive the economic waves but to use them to your advantage, enhancing your financial well-being no matter the economic weather.

Interactive Element: Economic Cycle Reflection Exercise

To deepen your understanding, take a moment to reflect on how the last economic cycle impacted your or your family's finances. What changes did you notice in your household income, job stability, or spending habits? Write these observations down and think about steps you could take now to better prepare for the next cycle.

15.2 HOW GLOBAL ECONOMICS AFFECTS YOUR WALLET

Global trade means countries are continually buying from and selling to each other. This interconnected market means the avocado you use in your morning toast could come from Mexico, while the phone in your hand was assembled in China with parts from Europe. It's a complex web of interactions, and when there's a shake-up in this system—say, a new tariff on steel imports or a ban on certain exports—it can shift the cost structures for a wide array of goods. For you, that might mean paying more for a car since the steel to build it costs more or noticing electronics prices have skyrocketed because of an increase in the cost of imported components.

Let's throw in some major international events like oil price shocks or trade wars. These are the heavyweights in the ring of global economics, and when they punch, they punch hard. Oil price fluctuations can be particularly jarring. Since oil is a cornerstone of most economies—fueling everything from cars to factories—an increase in oil prices can lead to higher costs for manufactured goods and transportation. This uptick can translate to your expenses, bumping up the cost of airline tickets, delivery services, and more. Similarly, a trade war, which happens when countries slap tariffs on each other's goods, can make imported items more expensive, leading to higher prices at the checkout line.

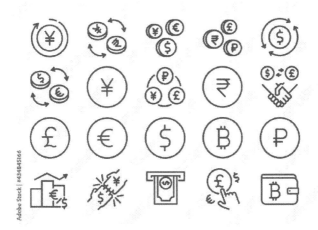

Being a savvy global consumer in this interconnected market means staying informed and agile. It's about understanding that the economic winds can shift, and so must your strategies for managing your money. For instance, if you hear about an impending trade policy that might hike up electronics prices, you might decide to buy that new laptop sooner rather than later.

In a world where economies are tightly linked, the ability to adjust to economic changes and plan for potential financial impacts can set you up for enduring success. Next, we will explore the intriguing world of ethical and sustainable finance.

CHAPTER 16

ETHICAL AND SUSTAINABLE FINANCE

I magine you've scored the ultimate job where you get paid to binge-watch your favorite shows and help script the next big hit. That's like ethical investing: you invest in companies that not only potentially grow your wealth but also contribute positively to the world. It's about adding a sprinkle of your values into your investment mix, ensuring that your money speaks the same language as your heart and conscience.

16.1 ETHICAL INVESTING: MAKING MONEY WHILE DOING GOOD

What's the scoop on ethical investing? It's not solely about avoiding companies that harm the planet or society; it's about supporting businesses making a positive impact. Think of it as the financial equivalent of choosing farm-to-table eateries over fast food chains. It feels good and makes a conscious choice that benefits a broader landscape.

What Is Ethical Investing?

Ethical investing means putting your money into companies and funds that align with your moral compass. That could involve industries like renewable energy, sustainable goods, or companies with reputable human rights and employee welfare. It's a way to ensure your investments contribute to advancements you believe in rather than supporting practices you oppose. In today's financial scene, it's a powerful statement about what you stand for, and it's gaining momentum faster than a superhero movie series.

How To Pick the Correct Ethical Investments

Start by diving into a company's practices and policies. Are they sourcing materials sustainably? Do they treat their workers well? What's their stance on corporate responsibility? Tools like ESG (Environmental, Social, and Governance) scores, which rate companies based on their ethical impact, are beneficial. They're like nutritional labels but for the moral value of your investments.

When it comes to where you can park your ethical investments, the landscape is rich and varied. ESG funds are a popular choice; these funds select stocks that meet strict ethical criteria, giving you a diversified portfolio.

Green bonds are designed to fund projects with positive environmental impacts, like renewable energy or pollution control. And let's not forget socially responsible mutual funds, which blend strong ethics with financial returns.

One of the biggest myths about ethical investing is that you sacrifice returns for morals. Not true. Recent studies suggest that companies focused on solid ESG principles often perform as well as, if not better than, their less scrupulous counterparts. The key lies in finding a balance that works for you and your investments.

Interactive Element: Ethical Investment Exploration Exercise

Spend time researching a company or fund aligning with your values. Check out their ESG score, read their latest sustainability report, and see what the financial experts say about their performance. That will give you a taste of ethical investing and empower you with the knowledge to make informed decisions about where your money goes.

Ethical investing is more than a trend; it's a movement toward a more conscious and sustainable financial future. It allows you to contribute to the causes you care about through the power of your investment dollars. Investing is about the future, and with ethical investing, it can be a future you're proud to be part of.

16.2 GREEN FINANCE: OPPORTUNITIES IN SUSTAINABLE INVESTING

You're ready to go green with your investments, and I'm not talking about planting a money tree in your backyard. Green finance is like the superhero of the financial world. It's all about channeling funds into projects that aim for a wallet-friendly return and make a solid thumbs-up impact on our planet. It's finance but with a green cape.

The Rise of Green Finance

Over the past few years, there's been a massive shift in how we think about investments. It's no longer about the greenbacks but also about how those bucks can battle climate change, reduce pollution, and promote sustainable practices. This wave of eco-conscious investing is driven by a growing recognition that environmental stability is crucial for our planet's health and economic stability. As more people, institutions, and governments prioritize sustainability, the flow of funds into green projects has surged, creating a robust market dedicated to environmental sustainability.

Green Bonds and Their Impact

Imagine green bonds as standard but with a twist: the funds raised are earmarked exclusively for projects with positive environmental benefits. That could be anything from developing renewable energy parks to boosting public transport to reduce carbon emissions. What's fantastic about green bonds is that they offer a way for investors to contribute to environmental projects while also receiving a return on their investment, just like traditional bonds. They are a tangible way to see your money making a direct positive impact on the environment.

Investing in Renewable Energy

This sector is like the blockbuster hit of green finance. With the world gradually turning away from fossil fuels, renewable energy projects—think solar panels, wind turbines, and hydroelectric plants—are seeing a surge in interest. Investing in this sector helps reduce the carbon footprint and taps into the growing demand for cleaner energy solutions. However, while the sun shines bright on renewable energy investments, it's vital to consider factors like technological advancements, regulatory changes, and market competition, which all influence the profitability and stability of these investments.

Evaluating Green Investments

Before you jump in, it's essential to do your homework. Just because an investment is labeled 'green' doesn't automatically make it a wise choice. Dig deeper. Look into the project's specifics: What environmental benefits does it promise? How feasible are these goals? Is the project backed by a solid plan and capable management? Also, check out the track record of the company or entity issuing the investment. Have they successfully undertaken and managed similar projects before? Are they financially stable? This due diligence is like being a detective in a mystery novel where you're piecing together clues to ensure that your investment yields returns and contributes to environmental sustainability.

Investing in green finance isn't only about watching your bank balance grow; it's about ensuring that your investments bring positive change in the world. As you explore these green opportunities, remember your financial choices shape the planet's future. Whether it's through bonds that fund clean water projects or stocks in cutting-edge renewable technology companies, your investment decisions foster a greener, more sustainable world.

Ready to put your money where your heart is? Let's make it happen.

16.3 ALIGNING YOUR FINANCIAL CHOICES WITH YOUR VALUES

Think about the last time you bought a birthday gift for someone you care about. You probably didn't just grab the first thing you saw on the shelf. More likely, you thought about what that person would appreciate—a gift that reflects their personality, likes, and values. Imagine applying the same thoughtful approach to your financial decisions. That is what it means to align your financial choices with your values. It's about how you spend, save, and invest your money, reflecting who you are and what you stand for.

When you start to view your financial decisions through the lens of your values, something amazing happens. Your choices feel more purposeful. You're no longer just saving money; you're funding your dreams. You're not just investing; you're planting seeds for a future that aligns with your vision of a better world. This kind of mindset shift can be incredibly empowering. It turns everyday financial decisions into powerful statements about what you believe in.

Impact Investing

Impact investing funds your money in companies or projects designed to generate social or environmental benefits alongside financial returns. Think of it as investing by valuing society, the environment, and your wallet. Imagine you're passionate about education. By investing in a company that provides affordable education solutions in underserved communities, you're contributing to the broader goal of increasing global education standards while aiming for a return on your investment. It's a win-win.

Impact investing isn't limited to global issues. It applies to the smaller, everyday choices that add up. Consider your choice of bank. Where you store your money can be a form of financial activism. Some banks use the money deposited with them to fund projects that might not align with your values—like fossil fuel extraction or manufacturing tobacco products. Others focus on lending to green technologies or social enterprises. By choosing a bank that invests in environmentally and socially responsible projects, you're effectively putting your money to work toward a better future, even while it sits in your account.

If this sounds like a strategy you want to adopt, you're probably wondering where to start. Luckily, there are resources to help you find investment options aligning with your values. Websites like Social Funds and GreenMoney provide detailed information on socially and environmentally responsible investing. They provide insights into different funds, the projects they invest in, and their performance. Tools like As You Sow can help you understand the impact of your current investments and find more aligned options.

This adventure through ethical and sustainable finance isn't simply about growing wealth; it's about increasing wealth with purpose. By choosing to invest ethically, engage in green finance, and align your financial decisions with your values, you're shaping a better world.

Carry with you the understanding that your financial choices have power. Use that power wisely and watch your investments transform.

Share Your Financial Freedom Journey!

Don't forget to use #FinancialFreedomJourney on social media and share your successes with the world. There's another way you can inspire more people like you to take this empowering journey as well – you can leave a review online.

Simply by sharing your honest opinion of this book and a little about your own journey so far, you'll inspire new readers to equip themselves with all the knowledge they need to set off on the road to financial freedom.

Thank you so much for your support. I can't wait to hear about your successes!

Scan QR code to leave review

CONCLUSION

Wow, what a ride we've been on together! From cracking open the vault on financial literacy to planting seeds for your future wealth and equity, we've covered serious ground. And let me tell you, the empowerment that comes from understanding your money? That's the jackpot.

Diving into the world of finances isn't just about padding your wallet (though that's a nice perk); it sets a rock-solid foundation for your financial future. Think of it like building a Lego mansion —you want to start with a strong base so that all the cool stuff you add later (like a Lego hot tub or a dragon-guarded tower) doesn't topple over.

We've journeyed through the essentials—mastering budgeting basics, harnessing the magic of saving, navigating the maze of credit and debt, laying down the roots with investing fundamentals, and let's not forget gearing up for those financial milestones. These aren't merely chapters in a book; they're your tools for building a fortress of monetary freedom.

Taking risks, managing your time like a boss, and working for yourself are attainable realities. With the proactive mindset we've fostered, you're ready to chase those dreams and make them your reality.

I won't sugarcoat it—this path has challenges, but guess what? Every hiccup is a chance to learn and grow stronger. Keep your eyes on the prize, and resilience is your best buddy.

Picture this: A future where you're not just surviving but thriving. Where financial worries are a thing of the past, and you have the freedom to pursue your passions and explore new horizons. That's not a dream; it's a destination, and you're well on your way.

So, what's next? Don't let this be the end. Take everything we've explored and put it into action. Start today—right now! Budget that allowance, save that birthday cash, invest in your ideas, and always plan for the next big thing.

And hey, don't go on this epic adventure alone. Share your story, your successes, and those oops moments. Use #FinancialFreedomJourney, and let's create a wave of financial savvy that inspires others.

Remember all those cool apps and resources we talked about? Keep them handy. They're your compass as you navigate your financial landscape.

From the bottom of my heart, thank you for joining me on this journey. I believe in you and your potential to achieve financial heights. Keep pushing, keep learning, and most importantly, keep dreaming. Here's to your future—may it be as bright and bold as you are.

Until our next financial adventure, Eduardo Hernandez.

REFERENCES

1. Happy State Bank. (n.d.). Six steps to creating a positive money mindset. *Happy State Bank.* https://www.happybank.com/resources/six-steps-to-creating-a-positive-money-mindset

2. Miller, K. (2023, June). How can behavioral science help our spending habits? 5 insights. *American Psychological Association.* https://www.apa.org/monitor/2023/06/psychology-of-spending

3. Charles Schwab & Co., Inc. (n.d.). SMART goals for your financial plan. *Schwab.* https://www.schwab.com/learn/story/smart-goals-your-financial-plan

4. Ramsey Solutions. (n.d.). How to set financial goals: 6 steps. *Ramsey.* https://www.ramseysolutions.com/personal-growth/setting-financial-goals

5. Marrs, K. (2023, May 12). Best budgeting apps for teens (I tried them all). *Kids' Money.* https://www.kidsmoney.org/teens/budgeting/apps/

6. Williams, A. (2023, May 26). The 50/30/20 budget rule explained with examples. *Investopedia.* https://www.investopedia.com/ask/answers/022916/what-502030-budget-rule.asp

7. Western & Southern Financial Group. (n.d.). Navigating an irregular income: Money management for unpredictable earnings. *Western & Southern.* https://www.westernsouthern.com/personal-finance/navigating-an-irregular-income

8. Omololu, E. (2024, March 15). 9 financial mistakes to avoid in your 20s and 30s. *Forbes.* https://www.forbes.com/sites/enochomololu/2024/03/15/9-financial-mistakes-to-avoid-in-your-20s-and-30s/

9. Charles Schwab & Co., Inc. (n.d.). Benefits of compound growth. *Schwab MoneyWise.* https://www.schwabmoneywise.com/essentials/benefits-of-compound-growth

10. Carmichael, C. (2023, June 27). 7 best round-up apps for saving + investing money instantly. *Nasdaq.* https://www.nasdaq.com/articles/7-best-round-up-apps-for-saving-investing-money-instantly-0

11. Forbes Advisor. (n.d.). Emergency fund calculator. *Forbes.* https://www.forbes.com/advisor/banking/emergency-fund-calculator/#:

12. Quicken. (2023, June 13). 12 fun summer money challenges for kids. *Quicken.* https://www.quicken.com/blog/challenges-for-kids/

13. Hall, T. (2023, July 7). How to read a pay stub. *Investopedia.* https://www.investopedia.com/how-to-read-your-paycheck-5094518

14. Hastings, E. (2023, December 28). 30 best side hustle ideas to earn extra cash in 2024. *Time.* https://time.com/personal-finance/article/best-side-hustles/

15. Ramsey Solutions. (n.d.). How to budget with an irregular income. *Ramsey.* https://www.ramseysolutions.com/budgeting/how-to-budget-an-irregular-income

16. Emen, J. (2022, July 6). How to negotiate your starting salary. *Harvard Business Review.* https://hbr.org/2022/07/how-to-negotiate-your-starting-salary

17. Hayes, A. (2023, June 22). What is a credit score? Definition, factors, and ways to improve it. *Investopedia.* https://www.investopedia.com/terms/c/credit_score.asp

18. Capital One. (n.d.). How to use a credit card responsibly: 10 tips. *Capital One.* https://www.capitalone.com/learn-grow/money-management/tips-using-credit-responsibly/

19. Wells, L. (2024, May 1). Pay off student loans fast with 7 strategies. *NerdWallet.* https://www.nerdwallet.com/article/loans/student-loans/pay-off-student-loans-fast

20. Forbes Advisor. (2024, May 2). How to prevent credit card fraud. *Forbes.* https://www.forbes.com/advisor/credit-cards/how-to-prevent-credit-card-fraud/

21. NerdWallet. (2024, May 5). Best brokers for beginners of May 2024. *NerdWallet.* https://www.nerdwallet.com/best/investing/online-brokers-for-beginners

22. Fidelity. (n.d.). Guide to diversification. *Fidelity.* https://www.fidelity.com/viewpoints/investing-ideas/guide-to-diversification

23. Horowitz, D. (2024, April 10). 8 common investing mistakes to avoid. *Investopedia.* https://www.investopedia.com/articles/stocks/07/beat_the_mistakes.asp

24. Sullivan, M. (2024, May 5). 10 best long-term investments in May 2024. *Bankrate.* https://www.bankrate.com/investing/best-long-term-investments/

25. FinIdeas. (2024, May 6). The importance of financial planning for young adults. *FinIdeas.* https://www.finideas.com/the-importance-of-financial-planning-for-young-adults/

26. MarketWatch. (2024, May 7). Life insurance considerations for millennials (2024 guide). *MarketWatch.* https://www.marketwatch.com/guides/insurance-services/life-insurance-considerations-for-millennials/

27. Maitz, J. (2024, April 15). Renting vs. buying a house: Which is right for you? *Bankrate.* https://www.bankrate.com/real-estate/renting-vs-buying-a-home/

28. LaPonsie, M. (2024, April 10). 5 popular investment strategies for beginners. *Bankrate.* https://www.bankrate.com/investing/investment-strategies-for-beginners/

29. Bank of America. (n.d.). How to file your own taxes: 6 steps for beginners. *Better Money Habits.* https://bettermoneyhabits.bankofamerica.com/en/taxes-income/how-to-file-your-taxes-in-your-20s

30. Forbes Advisor. (2024, May 10). Best tax software of May 2024. *Forbes.* https://www.forbes.com/advisor/taxes/tax-software/

31. Time Editorial Team. (2023, May 15). Roth IRA vs 401(k): What's the difference? *TIME Stamped.* https://time.com/personal-finance/article/roth-ira-vs-401k/

32. Internal Revenue Service. (2023, April 1). Common tax return mistakes that can cost taxpayers. *IRS.* https://www.irs.gov/newsroom/common-tax-return-mistakes-that-can-cost-taxpayers

33. Bautis Financial. (n.d.). The power of investing young: Use compound interest to build wealth. *Bautis Financial.* https://bautisfinancial.com/the-power-of-investing-young/

34. Investopedia Staff. (2024, February 12). 10 successful young entrepreneurs. *Investopedia.* https://www.investopedia.com/10-successful-young-entrepreneurs-4773310

35. NerdWallet. (2024, January 25). 17 best passive income ideas for 2024. *NerdWallet.* https://www.nerdwallet.com/article/investing/what-is-passive-income-and-how-do-i-earn-it

36. Picture Perfect Portfolios. (2023, November 5). FIRE case studies: Success stories of early retirement. *Picture Perfect Portfolios.* https://pictureperfectportfolios.com/fire-case-studies-success-stories-of-early-retirement/

37. Robinson, L., & Segal, J. (2024, March 4). Coping with financial stress. *HelpGuide.* https://www.helpguide.org/articles/stress/coping-with-financial-stress.htm

38. Laurie. (2023, December 10). Overcoming addiction to achieve emotional and financial resilience: A guest post by Laurie M. *Rich and Resilient Living.* https://www.richandresilientliving.com/overcoming-addiction-to-achieve-emotional-and-financial-resilience-a-guest-post-by-laurie-m/

39. ET Insights. (2023, October 2). Why is financial literacy important for young adults? *ET Insights.* https://etinsights.et-edge.com/why-is-financial-literacy-important-for-young-adults/

40. BluPeak Credit Union. (2023, August 7). Mind over money: 6 tips to reduce financial stress. *BluPeak.* https://www.blupeak.com/blog/mind-over-money-6-tips-to-reduce-financial-stress/

41. Finaciti. (2023, December 1). A comprehensive guide to top financial literacy apps of 2023. *Finaciti.* https://finaciti.com/best-financial-literacy-apps-2023-improve-money-management/

42. Federal Trade Commission. (2023, November 15). How to recognize and avoid phishing scams. *Consumer Advice.* https://consumer.ftc.gov/articles/how-recognize-and-avoid-phishing-scams

43. Bilyeu, T. (2023, September 8). The beginner's guide to crypto & NFTs. *Medium.* https://medium.com/@TomBilyeu/the-beginners-guide-to-crypto-nfts-d05c27cf0fd5

44. Kagan, J. (2024, February 14). Financial technology (fintech): Its uses and impact on our lives. *Investopedia*. https://www.investopedia.com/terms/f/fintech.asp

45. Para Team. (2024, March 2). 35 highest paying gig economy jobs: Gig apps that pay well. *WithPara*. https://www.withpara.com/blog/35-highest-paying-gig-economy-jobs

46. Gobler, E. (n.d.). How to budget with an irregular income. *Erin Gobler*. https://eringobler.com/budget-with-irregular-income/

47. Glover, R. (2023, June 2). Self-employed retirement plans: Know your options. *NerdWallet*. https://www.nerdwallet.com/article/investing/retirement-plans-self-employed

48. U.S. Small Business Administration. (n.d.). Write your business plan. *SBA*. https://www.sba.gov/business-guide/plan-your-business/write-your-business-plan

49. Gibbons, S. (2021, May 11). 8 strategies for lowering your startup costs. *Forbes*. https://www.forbes.com/sites/serenitygibbons/2021/05/11/8-strategies-for-lowering-your-startup-costs/

50. Capterra. (n.d.). Best financial management software for small businesses. *Capterra*. https://www.capterra.com/financial-management-software/s/small-businesses/

51. Startups.com. (n.d.). The 5 types of startup funding. *Startups.com*. https://www.startups.com/library/expert-advice/5-types-startup-funding

52. American Trading. (2023, September 14). How do consumers benefit from international trade? *American Trading*. https://www.american-trading.com/news/how-do-consumers-benefit-from-international-trade

53. Mitchell, C. (2023, February 15). Currency fluctuations: How they affect the economy. *Investopedia*. https://www.investopedia.com/articles/forex/080613/effects-currency-fluctuations-economy.asp

54. Kuepper, J. (2023, March 20). The risks of investing in emerging markets. *Investopedia*. https://www.investopedia.com/articles/basics/11/risks-investing-in-emerging-markets.asp

55. Hira, N. (2023, April 18). 7 ways to recession-proof your life. *Investopedia*. https://www.investopedia.com/articles/pf/08/recession-proof-your-life.asp

56. Chen, J. (2024, January 10). What is ESG investing? *Investopedia*. https://www.investopedia.com/terms/e/environmental-social-and-governance-esg-criteria.asp

57. PIMCO. (n.d.). Understanding green, social and sustainability bonds. *PIMCO*. https://www.pimco.com/gbl/en/resources/education/understanding-green-social-and-sustainability-bonds

58. B the Change Team. (2023, October 5). 15 companies making a difference with impact investing. *B the Change*. https://bthechange.com/15-companies-making-a-difference-with-impact-investing-9f3752774cc7

59. Carbon Collective. (n.d.). Renewable energy stocks: The complete guide to investing. *Carbon Collective*. https://blog.carboncollective.co/renewable-energy-stocks/